Fate of a Persian Boy

Mahmoud Izadi

London | New York

Published by Clink Street Publishing 2018

Copyright © 2018

First edition.

ISBN:
978-1-912850-29-7 - paperback
978-1-912850-30-3 - ebook

To my wife, Sheida

and Ghassan Shaker

Total Blackout

December 2nd 2015 was the sort of typically miserable, cold day that you can get in London at that time of year. Weather-wise there was nothing special about it in any way. But this particular day was to turn out like no other day I had ever encountered.

I had taken an old friend of mine, Harriet Crawley, to lunch at Queen's Club, the home of London's most prestigious sporting membership and famous for its pre-Wimbledon grass court tennis tournament. Having been a member there since the 1960s it was one of my favourite places in London and had also been the stage for my greatest ever sporting endeavour. It was great to see Harriet. She and I went way back – we had both been in Tehran thirty years earlier and for a long time she had gone out with one of my best friends. Sadly we had both had a fair share of tragedy in our lives but as always meeting up with her was a tonic and lit up my day. She was as tough as a nail but delightful as ever.

After a successful lunch we parted company and I went back home. I was confronted by an empty fridge, which was no great surprise as I had one more day before my wife, Sheida, was due back home from America. I decided to walk to the local Tesco's about half a mile away to get some provisions for later. Along the way I reflected on recent events in my life.

It had been so good to catch up with such a close old friend. I had lost four of my best friends within the last eight years and I missed them all terribly. I had always been too preoccupied with doing well in business, trying to be a good husband and

1

father, being a good friend and deriving pleasure from my love of sports to think about life and death too much. I was a happy-go-lucky person who felt very fortunate to be able to enjoy all the things in my life. My first marriage had sadly been a short union that hadn't worked out, but it had produced Nilu, my lovely daughter. But it was the death of my friends and the fact that I was now seventy-eight years old that had definitely got me thinking about where I was in my life.

As a boy I had been sent away from Tehran to boarding school in Norfolk because of the instability in Iran. At the time, the country had been divided up between the British and the Russians and nobody knew which way it was going to swing. Eventually the powers that be survived by getting rid of both of them. As an Iranian boy and therefore an outsider, I had suffered during the school experience, but I never blamed my parents or built up a hatred towards them for what they did. They thought that they had made the right decision and had got on with their lives in Iran, where it was a different life to many other countries post-war and there wasn't a shortage of anything. But I had felt abandoned and suffered as a result. Later at Cambridge, I made friends with others who had been through the same experience of being sent away to school. We all suffered from the same complexes when we met. The one thing that we loathed in our lives was abandonment and rejection.

But it wasn't just those thoughts that were on my mind. The truth of it was that I had been having rather darker thoughts of my own in recent months. I was beginning to ask myself some uncomfortable questions. I tended to speak what was on my mind and this was proving difficult to get to grips with. About a week previously, I had decided I needed to do something about it. I had wanted to find somewhere peaceful and quiet and then I remembered that I had been to the Roman Catholic Brompton Oratory church in Knightsbridge for various funerals. I thought it might be a good place to collect my thoughts. Growing up, my parents had been very devout in their Islamic faith. But I hadn't been sure what to think and used to mock God and religion because I couldn't believe in it. They used to tell me to shut up. 'He's listening!' But although I still had various issues with organised religion, at the same time I knew that I believed in God in my own way.

The church wasn't far from where I lived and so I made the short journey across London to pay it a visit. As I entered the imposing building I had felt good about things as I made my way to the front pew. I just sat there and looked at the cross and talked to God. It was very private and very emotional, but at the same time, rational. I wanted to know what was going on, why was it going on and where things were leading to. I kept asking him, 'What do you want from me?' I thought I had done everything prescribed in life to help my fellow human beings and I couldn't understand the response. After the conversation I had felt lighter and much stronger. It seemed to me that I had made a connection with God and I thought that somehow he had heard me. I still had questions that needed answering, but it had been such an uplifting experience and it had given me hope that I would find a way forward with my issues.

By now I was enjoying the short walk to the shops and felt that it must be doing me some good. I did my shopping and then headed back for home. I was aware of a few people around me as I crossed from Cromwell Rd into Warwick Rd. I was looking forward to seeing Sheida and wondered what time–

BANG!

Total blackout.

Dad

- *Nilu* -

I had been in church attending a Christmas carol service with my young son Max for about twenty minutes when something made me look at my phone. It was switched on to silent mode and was lying face down on the pew beside me. I picked it up and checked the screen. Twenty-five missed calls. Something had clearly happened.

At the same a text came in from my husband Greg saying, 'Nilu, your father has been hit by a van but he's okay.' I played a voicemail message and it was from a police officer explaining what had happened to him but also saying that he was fine. I discovered via another message that they had taken him to St Mary's Hospital in Paddington.

I wanted to see my father as soon as possible but I now had some quick decisions to make. It was 8 pm on a winter's night with Christmas shopping having started, rush hour not having yet finished and I was across town in Chelsea with my four-year-old son Max.

It was tricky. I really didn't know what to do. Should I take Max to the hospital? How would I get to the hospital? Should I go by car? I was an hour away from my own home, it was getting late and with the shock of the news I was feeling overwhelmed.

Thankfully my brother-in-law John stepped in and we agreed that given the circumstances, he would kindly take Max and me to the hospital. We started our journey, fighting against all the traffic and the shoppers and finally arrived at the hospital. As I entered A&E, a police officer took me aside.

'It wasn't your father's fault. No matter where you are crossing or how, it's not the pedestrian's fault,' he said. I didn't quite know what he meant and it seemed a slightly odd thing to say. Besides I had been told that Dad was okay. St Mary's was busy, but I found out where he was and the three of us proceeded to make our way to see him.

He was not okay. He was lying on a stretcher covered in blood and not in a fit state to be seen by a four-year-old. I felt frustrated that we hadn't been given the correct information. John managed to whisk Max off to another area and keep him entertained, no mean feat in such an environment, whilst I went about finding out as much as I could about what had happened.

Nobody seemed to know the full story and I kept on discovering snippets of information. Apparently my father had been hit by an SUV and thrown fifteen feet into the air on impact. Cromwell Rd had been cordoned off for two hours and closed around the area of the accident. The air ambulance had been called and landed next to the site. After an initial assessment the paramedics had decided that the best course of action was for my father to be taken to hospital by road.

But frustratingly, I couldn't seem to get much information about the extent of his injuries. Instead, I was given a plastic bag full of his personal belongings. I opened it up to find it contained his watch, phone and wallet as well as all the clothes that he had been wearing. It was incredibly upsetting going through everything. It was all covered in blood and his clothes were in pieces where they had cut him out of them. It was disgusting and I felt sick. Later on I would have to throw most of his clothes away although I would be able to save his scarf. As I went through his things I thought about him as a father and what we meant to each other.

Our relationship had always been based on humour and we had always enjoyed each other's company. I had never really used him as a confidante, but he had always been a very loving person and was a fantastic raconteur and great fun to be around. I guess the best years of our lives were going to the football together. When I left college I was twenty-five and feeling slightly spare. So to do something about that I started accompanying my father to watch Arsenal every Saturday from 1998 to 2003. We would always meet at Barons Court station. Same station, same outfit: coat, hat and scarf. We would get to Arsenal's stadium, Highbury, half an hour early and would go to the local burger joint before the match. It became our little father and daughter tradition and was the highlight of the week. And then we would take our seats in the East Stand Upper and watch football, just father and daughter together. My father would mispronounce words quite a lot, to the extent that one of our fellow supporters, a famous cultural TV broadcaster of the time was forever referred to as Mervyn and not Melvyn. I'm not sure whether it was deliberate on his part or not, but a bond between us was cemented in a wonderful five year period going to see Arsenal play. Those were the best years of our life for Dad and me. Fine art was my passion at the time but football became our common interest.

I came back to the real world and managed to compose myself. Still wanting to find out more information, I went to speak to Dad who at this point seemed frail, but well in himself.

'Hi darling, they wanted your number and I gave it to them,' he told me. Which was amazing for the fact that he remembered my phone number! But something was not quite right. And clearly there were some crossed wires because when my husband had spoken to the police officer he had been assured that he was okay. And now I was being told by the medical staff that he *was* okay, but that he had had an impact to his head and they were worried about an internal bleed. It was all a bit confusing and I could see with the number of doctors and nurses attending him and the various tests being done that things were not as simple as we had been led to believe. I needed to get hold of Sheida and let her know what was happening.

BY HIS SIDE

- Sheida -

I was due to fly back from Miami, arriving in London on December 3rd. I was putting everything in the car in preparation for the drive to the airport when I had a call from my son-in-law Jake. He had been informed by Nilu that her father – and my husband, Mahmoud – had been involved in a car accident and had been taken to St Mary's Hospital in Paddington.

I told Jake that I was on my way to the airport as I was flying out that evening and due to get into London the following morning. I asked him if he was going to see Mahmoud and he replied that he was and would Skype me so I could talk to him.

Mahmoud had been admitted to the trauma ward and was sitting on the bed when I finally got to speak with him on the phone. He looked in quite a state and I was shocked by his appearance. But of course it was also good just to see him and hear him talking. Nilu his daughter was there with him as well.

'How are you?' I asked him.

'Don't worry about me, the car hit me but I'm fine,' he replied.

It was a relief to hear this but then I asked him what he was doing there and he just went blank. He couldn't seem to remember. Naturally, this concerned me but I tried not to let it show. He repeated that he was fine and I said okay, perfect and that I would see him tomorrow at the hospital.

'Have a good flight,' he said to me. And that was the end of our conversation. But I managed to speak to Nilu out of his earshot and asked her what had happened. She told me everything that she knew and when I heard that they had called out an air ambulance, deep down I thought that things must be quite serious.

I put down the phone. I was in shock and couldn't wait to catch my flight and get back to London. It had been a relief to talk to him and hear that he was okay. But I needed to get to the hospital to see Mahmoud for myself. One thing in particular was bothering me. There seemed to be a lack of information about any injuries Mahmoud might have and how they might have affected him. This I'm sure was bad enough if you were at the hospital but I had an eight and a half hour transatlantic journey to deal with before I could get there. It was going to be a long flight.

I boarded the plane and as I took my seat, my stress levels began to rise and I actually got quite scared. I had so many thoughts running through my head. Why had they closed Cromwell Rd? What was going to happen to him overnight? Was he really okay? What if it was really serious? I needed to try and take my mind off things. I thought back to when I had first met Mahmoud in 1999. I was running a small designer fashion business at the time and he was this charming man who was just so full of life, joie de vivre. He had invited me to his tennis club and we had bonded over a love of tennis. He was a very good player and was always looking to be active. Whether it was playing sport or socialising he was not the type just to sit at home and always wanted to be doing something.

He was also quite the ladies' man and still wanted to stay friends with his old girlfriends. He had been single for many years when we first met and was leading the bachelor lifestyle. I think he would have been quite happy to keep that style of life but still have a partner! But it was all part of his charm. Once we had both retired we travelled extensively together, visiting France and Italy in particular, as well as the United States.

The thoughts helped me for a while, but then my worries began to resurface. I knew I needed to get some rest for what lay ahead but my mind was racing with too many uncertainties to be able to sleep. I had to find a solution. Normally I had two choices. I would either take a Melatonin tablet which helped me sleep and also deal with any jetlag. Or I would have a couple of glasses of red wine. I never mixed the two together. But on that night I did. I knew that I needed to be strong and full of energy for when I arrived.

The next thing I knew I was waking up to sunlight shining through the cabin windows. I had slept for virtually the whole flight. As I was coming to, I somehow had this feeling that Mahmoud would not be able to talk to me. It was a very strong feeling, almost like a sixth sense.

My daughter Samira picked me up from Heathrow airport and drove me directly to St Mary's Hospital. When we arrived I went straight to see him, but as I got to the trauma ward, I discovered that his condition had worsened overnight. Mahmoud was lying on a bed and I greeted him as I approached but he didn't open his eyes. I tried again as I reached his bedside.

'What happened?' I said to him. He shrugged. 'Can you hear me?' I continued. He responded by squeezing my hand. He was trying hard but he was clearly having difficulty breathing and it was making it difficult to communicate.

I was told by the doctors that overnight he had undergone a series of tests including an MRI scan, various x-rays and blood tests, but that they still had no idea how severe the internal injuries were and were awaiting more results.

The trauma ward was getting more and more frantic. Everyone was rushing around with various doctors and nurses coming and going. It was difficult to understand what exactly was going on. We would get a brief update saying they were investigating the seriousness of his injuries and he appeared to be in good hands, but it was frustrating not to be able to speak to someone and get a definitive answer as to what had happened to him. I wondered whether he was going to be okay and what was going to happen next.

By the afternoon I had my answer. Mahmoud's condition had deteriorated. At the same time we were getting more and more information as the results of his tests were coming through. With each one I began to understand how critical the situation was. His spine was broken but we were told he had actually been incredibly lucky. The spine had broken in a certain way, whereas breaking the other way would have meant that he would have been paralysed. If there was a best way to break a back Mahmoud had somehow managed it!

But any joy was short-lived as news was coming through that he had a whole list of other injuries. The car had hit him on the left-hand side of his body and he had fallen on that side as well. So every part of the left-hand side of his body was completely broken. Starting with his head he had suffered a brain haemorrhage. His left arm was damaged and he had broken and badly cut his thumb. He had a fractured pelvis, a fractured rib, a punctured lung and a shattered left knee.

It was a lot of information to take in all at once but something even more serious was now happening. His breathing difficulties had reached a critical level and were causing him to hyperventilate. It was a very worrying moment and the doctors informed me that because of his injuries they had to do something about it immediately.

He was rushed to the ICU (Intensive Care Unit) where he was intubated. This was a medical procedure where they inserted a flexible endotracheal tube into his mouth, past his vocal chords and down into his trachea to help ventilate his lungs and assist his breathing. The procedure seemed to go well and after a while I was told that he had stabilised. I asked one of the doctors what had happened and he replied that because Mahmoud's fractured rib had punctured his lungs he had been at huge risk of blood accumulating in the lungs and could have died at any moment.

Mahmoud was now in an induced coma and he lay there prostrate on the bed. For a moment the ward was quiet and after all the urgency, it felt like a calmness had descended. I hadn't really had time to gather my senses since I had arrived and I just sat there beside him watching him breathe through this tube. In and out, in and out. It was a strange sensation seeing him like this. He looked serene, but in a way quite lifeless.

The Other World

I was so full of energy! I was still Mahmoud but it seemed like this great life source was pulsating through me and I felt vibrant, strong and positive. And yet calm and peaceful at the same time. I appeared to the best possible version of me and truly hadn't felt this good in years. I couldn't believe how fantastic I was feeling. I didn't where I was or what exactly I was doing. In fact there were lots of things that I didn't know. But the one thing that I did know was that right now, it was very good to be me.

It was night-time and I was standing by the side of a road. I couldn't really appreciate my immediate surroundings but it felt as though I was waiting to go somewhere. Before I knew it, I became aware of a beautiful sports car approaching and I watched it as it pulled up to where I was standing. I looked inside and saw that it was being driven by a well-dressed, handsome man. It was Nasser Safari. We were very close and it was great to see him but what was he doing here? At that moment it didn't seem to matter. He was accompanied by a beautiful female companion dressed in red. We acknowledged each other and exchanged silent pleasantries.

Without any words being spoken, it appeared that they were offering me a lift. Before I really knew what was happening, I found myself getting into the car. Where were we going? I wasn't sure. But somehow it just seemed the right thing to do and I was happy to go with the flow. Our journey began and as Nasser drove, I thought how wonderful but strange it was to see him in this world.

Nasser was my cousin and his mother was my mother's sister. A very astute businessman, he had earned his fortune by building up a hugely successful steel business. He had a great reputation in the industry and had become the steel industry's leading figure by contracting all the major agencies for one of the first new steel mills that had been built in Iran. A very kind and extremely generous man we were more than just cousins, he was one of my closest friends in the world. But at one point in our lives we had hardly known each other.

When the Iranian revolution had taken place, Nasser, like many others, had come to live in London. He used to invite a group of friends to lunch every day at the Carlton Hotel and then later they would go back to his flat in Belgravia and play cards. At the time I lived in nearby Rutland Gate, but I wasn't part of his social gatherings. I knew that he was also a keen tennis player but we didn't really spend any time together, although living nearby I would occasionally bump into him and we would exchange pleasantries. Our conversations were always perfectly cordial, but somehow we hadn't made that connection with one another that you need to in order to become close friends.

Then one day he called me out of the blue and asked if I was attending the famous Stella Artois tennis tournament at Queen's Club where I was a member. I told him that yes I was going and invited him as a guest. I made sure that we sat in the best part of the stand to watch the tennis, introducing him to various friends throughout the day and we had a wonderful time enjoying the club's hospitality. A few days later he contacted me again and asked if I could propose him as a member. He had fallen in love with Queen's Club.

At that time, the chairman, Anthony Ward, was a great friend of mine. But he had never met Nasser, didn't know anything about him and with Queen's being such a prestigious sporting club, membership was a sought after commodity. But I approached Anthony regardless and put the proposal to him.

'Well,' he replied, going on to say in that quaint English way of validating someone, 'if he's *your* cousin Mahmoud, I suppose he's alright…' Nasser received his prized membership of the club within twenty-four hours. I had introduced him to a new world and it was the beginning of a great friendship. After that our relationship became unstoppable. Every time he came to London he would come to play tennis at Queen's and we would go out to dinner afterwards.

And here he was now, helping me on a journey to an unknown destination. It was very kind of him but surreal at the same time. We hadn't been driving very long when all of a sudden we came to a halt. It appeared that we had reached a stopping point, so I got out of the car. I felt like I had been taken from one place to another, but in a way that I didn't fully yet understand. I watched the car drive off and Nasser disappear back to where he had come from. It seemed like he had delivered me to a place for the next stage of my journey. Was he now returning the favour and introducing me to my new world?

I looked around to get my bearings and realised that I was in front of a beautiful tavern-style restaurant. I decided to enter it. Inside, the decor was stunning, with this incredible, intricate wooden panelling and an amazing high ceiling. It appeared to be busy, with high-end customers at every table, but I couldn't really make any of them out. I was standing there just taking in the whole scene when I heard a familiar voice cut through the ambient noise.

'About time you showed up.' I turned around and couldn't believe my eyes. There at a table in front of me were my four best friends from my Cambridge days: Foulad Hadid, Janeau Khayat, Piero Roberti and Parviz Radji. Grinning back at me, they were clearly enjoying the surprised look on my face and more comments quickly followed.

'Where have you been?'

'We haven't seen you for a long time.'

'Thank God you're here. We've been waiting for you.'

I laughed and we embraced. I was really overwhelmed to see them. I wasn't sure what I was expecting to happen in this strange new world but I certainly wasn't expecting to see any of my Cambridge cohorts.

Janeau was an amazing character. A Palestinian, he spoke about seven languages fluently. He loved affluence and wouldn't settle for anything but the best. He was the greatest entertainer at any party and used to get up and sing romantic songs in different languages. Because of his love of the good things in life and his ability to charm and make people feel good about themselves, he was hugely popular and kept everyone entertained with his songs and dancing, not to mention his outstanding intellect. Friends with the powerful and wealthy, he was invited to the best parties and social occasions around the world. After the revolution, I had become a close friend of Princess Fatima, the youngest sister of the Shah. She always made quite an impression on those who were lucky enough to meet her and I certainly went up in Janeau's estimation as a result. Of medium height, he was very good looking and always with a smile on his face. But behind the happy front that he presented to the world, he was actually quite a tragic character, with an unhappy marriage to one of Germany's wealthiest women.

Beside him was Piero Roberti, an Italian count, he was the known as the 'King of San Marino' and moved in high society – his mother had remarried Peter Thorneycroft the Chancellor of the Exchequer. A great friend, Piero had been two years above me at Cambridge and then became my neighbour in London where we saw each *sans cesse*. I went to Italy many times to visit him. After Cambridge he got a job with Eni, an Italian oil company. And one morning, the company's chairman rang his house asking for him.

'Can I speak to Count Roberti?' he asked.

'How dare you wake up the count at this time of the day, he's asleep,' came the reply from Piero's faithful maid. He was one of my best friends but I'm not sure that he ever worked a day in his life! He had enough money to get by and married Elizabeth Stauffenberg whose family name was well known in that her uncle, Claus Von Stauffenberg, had been one of the German conspirators who tried to assassinate Hitler during the war. Piero was slim, tall and with piercing blue eyes and was one of the most loyal friends a man could have. I used to invite him to play tennis at Queen's for which he was always very grateful and we would meet up at Montpeliano's in London. A quiet character he used to sit in the corner, smoke a packet of cigarettes and never say a word. And he never, ever, drank water.

Foulad Hadid was larger than life and my closest friend from Cambridge. We were just on the same wavelength. Another multi-linguist, he was probably the best dressed man at the university. A good-looking Iraqi he liked nothing better than making jokes, although normally at someone else's expense. A great sportsman, we used to play tennis and had many fantastic adventures as we travelled the world together. We had shared a flat together for five years after Cambridge when I was working in London. They were some of the happiest years of my life. He married Princess Kenza, the niece of the King of Morocco and had a palace in Cabo Negro, Morocco where I used to go and stay every summer. In later life he wrote the memoirs of his father, a prominent Iraqi politician, as well as becoming a fellow of St Antony's College, Oxford.

Parviz Radji made up the four. An Iranian, he was a year ahead of me at Cambridge. Charm personified, he became the Shah's last ambassador in London. A great tennis player and golfer he married a very good friend of mine Goli. Parviz was very loyal and we were the kind of friends who would just see each for a few hours every so often. Our friendship was cemented by a stand he took against a very powerful Iranian where he defended my name and honour. To him, loyalty and truth far outweighed any 'political gain' he might have made with someone who was so influential.

These were my best friends from my Cambridge days. But there was just one problem. Or four problems to be exact. Janeau had died in Acapulco ten years ago, the victim of suffering a stroke at the wheel of his car. I was sixty-nine at the time and we were all incredibly shocked when we heard the news. I remembered going to a memorial service at a church in Knightsbridge and seeing his two sons and the look on their faces as they processed what had happened to their father.

Piero had died of cancer of the bladder in Gstaad. Nobody knew he had been suffering from cancer as he had kept it to himself. He had gone to stay in Gstaad for the winter, but had ended up staying for the summer because he was in too much pain to face walking up the steps to his home in Rutland Gate. The next thing that I had heard was that he was dead.

Foulad had died of cancer of the lung. We had been inseparable. We shared a great friend in Ghassan Shaker and Ghassan would visit his grave whenever he came to London. Finally Parviz, the Shah's last ambassador in London, had died of cancer of the lung as well.

These were my closest friends and I had known them for well over half of my lifetime. And yet here they were now standing in front of me and acting as though it was only a few weeks since we had all seen each other. It was if nothing had changed. It should of course have been unbelievable but somehow it wasn't and I just went with the flow. I knew that not one of them happened to be still alive! So where exactly was I? What was going on? I really had no idea. But in this exact moment, it did not seem to matter and we sat down and picked up as though nothing had changed. We ordered great food, great wine and had a fantastic time.

But when the dinner was over something strange happened. I suddenly found myself in a different place. It was hard to understand what had happened. I wasn't transported exactly, it was just that one minute I was in one place and the next minute, well, in another.

I was now in a bedroom inside this house. I had no idea how I had got there and it was very disconcerting. I felt incredible in myself, like a new me, but not knowing what was happening felt very strange and surreal. After meeting up with my friends and now finding myself in this new environment, I decided I needed to find out some answers. So I got up from my bed and went downstairs. As I looked around the house I realised that the rooms looked familiar as did the furnishings. And then all of a sudden it clicked as to why I recognised everything. To my utter amazement, I realised that I was in my old house in Daroos in northern Tehran.

I explored my surroundings further. I looked inside my bedroom closet and found that all my clothes were hanging up and were ready for me to wear. Inside the kitchen and around the dining area I discovered plates of amazing food had been laid out and were ready for me to eat. In the sitting room I noticed that there was a telephone which raised the question of whether I should try and call someone. But I didn't know how to get in contact with anyone. And then a flash of colour caught my eye. I wandered over to a large window and looking through it I was stunned by what I saw in front of me. It was a magnificent garden, full of beautiful, exotic plants with insects buzzing around them and colourful birds flying back and forth across a clear blue sky. A river meandered through the greenery and in the middle of it was a wonderful swimming pool that looked incredibly inviting. It was a truly wonderful scene and I just stood there taking in the extraordinary spectacle. But there was one thing missing from this idyllic scenario. The garden was empty except for all the animals. And I had noticed that there was no evidence of anyone else around, either inside or outside. Who had made all the food for me to eat? Who had laid out all my clothes? Where exactly was everybody? I decided to take stock of my situation. When I had seen my friends I felt that somehow I had joined them. Although there was something strange about our interaction which I couldn't quite put my finger on. Had I died? Was this heaven? It was certainly a heavenly place. And I knew that my friends had died. I was absolutely certain of that. I could see by their reactions that I must have been visibly shocked when I had seen them. It was hardly a surprise. They were supposed to be *dead* after all. But they had greeted me as a true friend and it was fantastic to see them after such a long time apart. And they had made no mention of my death. They just said that they were pleased to see me.

So it was all quite confusing on the one hand but wonderfully clear and simple on the other. I was in an incredible place and felt truly amazing. I just wanted to give in to the incredible surroundings and enjoy every moment. Maybe I had transcended. It was definitely odd. Since I had been in this place it had felt like I was embracing organic life through every sense. But even so, I knew that I didn't quite feel fully part of it.

The whole scenario was unbelievable. I couldn't take my eyes off everything around me. My house seemed familiar, but nothing else in particular. But that didn't matter. The beautiful scenery was vividly green. Nature was abundant and just incredibly pure. I just stood there in awe and complete admiration of it all. It was like I was an observer but in the best ever place and not in any world that I had known before. It felt like paradise. I had never known such peace and tranquillity. I had never felt so happy. I seemed to have escaped the only world that I knew and this was an infinitely better place. I had no real anxiety here. No fear of anything. For a moment I thought it was almost dreamlike but it just felt too real for that.

The tranquillity was rudely interrupted by a ringing sound. It was the doorbell to my house. Someone was at the door. Intrigued to find out who was there, I opened it and was met by a grinning Parviz Radji.

'I'm here,' he said.

So this is how things worked in this place. I hadn't seen Nasser since the car journey, but here was Parviz once again, acting as though everything was completely normal. Well it didn't feel very normal to me! But it was definitely good to see another person again and especially an old friend. We warmly embraced and I left my house and followed him as we headed towards his car. But despite the beauty that surrounded me and despite the utter peace and tranquillity that enveloped me, a thought kept on running through my head. Why was I here?

Divine Intervention

- *Sheida* -

The medical staff in St Mary's had been fantastic, but now Mahmoud was in this induced coma and he had entered the realm of the unknown. Every day I would visit the hospital and when I saw him, I would talk to him and then squeeze his hand to see if there was any feeling. I wanted to see if I could get a response but there never was. So I would go and see the doctors to check on what progress was being made. But this was not enough for me and I knew I wanted to do something else to try and help him.

Because of my strong Muslim faith I have a small Koran that I always carry with me in my handbag. The Koran is a sacred text which is the primary source of every Muslim's faith and practice. I spoke to the doctor and told them that I wanted to use the Koran and my faith to help Mahmoud and would they have any objections if I placed the Koran with him and left it there? They said that was absolutely fine and so I started the process by putting my Koran under his pillow. I then decided that I would place it directly over his most severe injuries to try and help them heal directly. I started with his head for the blood clot on his brain. Taking the Koran in hand I kissed it leaving a lipstick mark whilst praying to God and my faith and asking him to give Mahmoud another chance. I then lowered the Koran onto the area of his head where the doctors had told me the damage was and ever so lightly touched it and in effect massaged the area. I sealed my prayer to God by then kissing the Koran. I then moved down to his damaged lung and repeated the actions. Every time I went out of the ICU to have a break or get a cup of coffee, upon my return I would go through the same process. To change things around a little I would then perform the process every hour or so. I continued doing this day after day until it just became part of my routine during my daily visit.

Because of all his injuries Mahmoud had a huge number of specialists and consultants who would come in and check up on how each specific injury was doing and what next treatment was needed. He had lung and heart specialists, an orthopaedic consultant and a neurologist, as well as all the nurses and back-up members of the team. He had so many major issues that it seemed like it was difficult to decide which one should take priority. But one of the issues that now really concerned them was his spine. The impact during the accident had crushed it. Mahmoud couldn't move his body and he was getting bad bed sores as a result. They needed to operate on it but at the same time they needed to address the bleeding in his lung caused by the fractured rib piercing it. They had been draining the lung up to now but now an operation was seen as a necessity. The lung specialist showed me how they would were going to open up his body on his left side near his lung. They were going to use a magnetic metallic instrument because they couldn't operate and use their hands as they might do usually. The magnetic instrument would lift the fractured ribs from his lung which would allow him to breathe and give him a better chance of survival.

But there was a problem. Because of his condition under the induced coma they weren't sure whether it was safe to operate or not. Leave things as they were and Mahmoud's breathing although stabilised, wouldn't get any better and his condition could only get worse. But if they operated and there were complications due to the nature of the rib piercing the lung he might not make it out of the operating theatre. It really was a Catch-22 situation.

Each new day they would discuss the decision and go back and forth about whether to perform the operation or not. At the same time they consulted with Nilu and myself and informed us about the pros and cons of the operation. They were worried about Mahmoud's age because of course he wasn't a young man and any major operation was always a risk. Of course the delay in making a decision only added to the tension and despite their professionalism and expertise, I was getting really worried about what the eventual outcome was going to be. The 'will they won't they' scenario was becoming a daily torture and it got to the point where still not knowing was almost as stressful as hearing any bad news. The team in the ICU were doing an incredible job, but I thought that at some point they were just going to have to make a decision. Unless we were all just hoping for something incredible to happen. And then one day, six days after he had entered the coma, it did.

As a matter of course, Mahmoud's condition was being monitored on a daily basis, with various tests and x-rays being conducted. This particular day, I was by his side when the lung specialist came in and told me he wanted to show me something. He produced the latest x-ray that had been taken of the lung area.

It showed that something incredible was indeed happening. The fractured ribs were lifting out of the lung by themselves. He couldn't believe it. After all their deliberation about what to do, he said the problem had resolved itself. I was overjoyed although I wasn't sure that I agreed with him that the problem had 'just resolved itself'. I believed that there had been a different form of intervention. A true miracle. What else could it be?

It was the first real breakthrough that we had had since Mahmoud had been admitted to the hospital. After everything that had happened and all the uncertainty, it was a relief to finally get some good news. Little did I know that it was only the first of many challenges that we were all going to face.

A Persian Boy

I was with Parviz in his car. I didn't know where we were going and I still didn't know why I was here, but as we drove along the incredible sensory overload I was experiencing and the familiarity of some of the things from my past put me in a reflective mood. I began to think about what I had done and where I had been in my life. This strange new world that I was now in was not the first time I had entered an unexpected world. But there was a big difference between the two experiences. My entry into this world had so far been amazing in every way, whereas my first journey into a strange world had been anything but.

It was 1947, I was nine years old and my elder brother and I were being sent to school in England. I had barely been out of Tehran before, let alone travel to another country. Our parents waved us off at the airport and being September, the weather in Tehran was beautiful as our plane took off and we climbed up into the clear blue skies. I was ready to embark on a great big adventure and it felt even more exciting due to the fact that I had not always found things that easy in my short life so far.

At five months old I had caught pneumonia. The doctors had told my mother to be prepared for the fact that I wasn't going to survive. But somehow I had pulled through. As a result of the illness I was a very feeble and weak child. At school I was dying to be an athlete and a runner, but I just wasn't good enough. I was full of enthusiasm, but I couldn't perform how I wanted to. I just didn't have the body to carry me. I had a bony chest known as a pigeon chest, that stuck out because I was so weak. It was soul-destroying because deep down I knew I was as good as the other children, I just couldn't prove it. It was very frustrating. But I didn't complain about my troubles, I just suffered in silence.

Our aeroplane journey took us via Beirut, Cairo, Paris and finally to London. We were collected by my uncle who brought us into the centre of the capital. It was quite a shock. The whole city seemed very grey and stank of pollution. We passed a lot of bomb sites which were scary and the trams in the middle of the street loomed up on us and seemed like they could run you over at any second. The whole place seemed very unfriendly. Not to my mention that to my young eyes, the people I saw around me did not appear to be very happy.

Although the availability of food was still restricted in post-war London, my poor uncle had managed to save my brother and me a boiled egg each from his rations. We ate them in silence, unsure about this strange new world. We stayed the night in his flat in Kensington and as I tried to fall asleep, I wondered what I was getting myself into.

The next day he took us to Liverpool St station. It was full of the hustle and bustle of London life, but because I could only speak rudimentary English and just use simple words like 'come', 'go' or 'yes', every encounter felt new and alienating. We boarded a train and began another journey. After several hours we reached what was then known as Norwich Thorpe station. By now I was terrified, as I didn't know where to go or what to do. But at least I still had my brother with me.

We were met by an elderly couple – the headmaster of our soon to be new school and his wife. They picked us up in their car and we started the ten mile drive to the school. As I looked out of the backseat window, what struck me was the total greenery of the Norfolk fields and countryside. I had never seen anything so green in my life.

Finally, we turned off the road, drove through some gates and headed up a long driveway. As we did so, this huge edifice loomed in front of us. This was Langley School and was to be our new home. We pulled up to the building and were taken inside, but once there, we were in for a shock. The school was virtually empty. There were certainly no other boys around. Unfortunately my father had sent us to school a week before term had started. It felt like nobody knew quite what to do with us and we were shoved into a massive dormitory and left to our own devices. It was a huge space full of empty beds and we both gravitated towards the middle of it. Exhausted and disorientated, we huddled together and howled and screamed for our parents, but they were thousands of miles away and nobody could hear our cries. Even with my brother there beside me, I had never felt so alone.

Nothing really seemed to happen in the first few days of us being there. On one occasion we were shown the school chapel with its endless rows of gravestones. I had never seen gravestones before and wasn't sure that I liked being around them and found the whole thing pretty unsettling. I think they thought it might somehow cheer us up, but it just made our situation worse and I felt traumatised. Eventually, an Austrian boy, Freddie Bettelheim, another with parents in absentia, was assigned to us and began to teach us better English. And we were each given bicycles, which we used to explore the grounds. But this new country was cold and I felt isolated and miserable.

And then one day, about a week later, a few cars arrived at the school, followed by more and more. School term had finally started. At last we would have some other boys around us for company. But their arrival didn't guarantee to make our lives better. The other boys had never seen foreigners before and thought that my brother and I were a couple of extraterrestrials! It was hard to keep going and be positive, but somehow my brother and I fought through it together.

And then came the moment that changed everything. Rugby started and every boy was to participate. I didn't actually know how to play but I was looking forward to it. Despite my previous sickness, I still believed in myself. I knew I just needed a chance to prove it. But because my brother was two years older than me, we were chosen to play in different teams. Now I really was on my own.

The game began and I watched the others to try and learn what to do. I saw someone else score try and I realised that that was the object of the game. A few minutes later I got hold of the ball about thirty yards from the touchline. And suddenly it was as if everything in my life so far just came together in an instant. The pneumonia, the strange new country, the separation from my parents – all of it had somehow led to me standing there on a pitch with a rugby ball in my hands. I knew what I had to do. This was my moment and I took it. I ran and I didn't stop. As I did so, the other boys just seemed to fall away from me and I scored a try. The feeling was incredible. So the next time I got the ball, I did it again.

I had earned some respect amongst my peers with my sporting exploits but I still wanted a few other aspects of my life to improve. One of them was the food. It was so mundane and seemed to consist of just mashed potato with everything. The puddings were no better, with both tapioca and semolina standing out but in no way being a highlight. I was now playing sport the whole time and so was constantly hungry. And then one day I saw some of the other boys eating jam sandwiches. They were day boys and with my newfound status I found it easy to befriend them. Before long they were asking their mothers to make extra jam sandwiches for me which they duly did. I didn't go hungry again.

Things got a bit better after that. I wasn't to see my mother for another three years and my father for another two years. But my adventure had begun and I was ready for anything.

7% Chance of Survival

– *Sheida* –

Although the 'rib healing' had gone well, Mahmoud was by no means out of danger. Despite the successful outcome I still had plenty of other concerns. The consultants were now considering whether they should proceed with the spine operation, but were concerned about his head injury. A scan had showed that a huge blood clot had formed on his brain and there was a discussion between the various consultants as to how to treat it. One of them suggested that they needed to drain the blood, but another disagreed saying that when you drained the blood, the area of drainage could become empty, leading to complications. I was concerned as to which way they would go but I had to trust their judgement in making the right decision. And something else had arisen that made things even more complicated.

Mahmoud had been born with only one functional kidney. In everyday life this was not seen as any kind of issue, but because of his injuries, he had had a catheter inserted into his kidney to drain his urine and I was worried about whether it was damaged. He had obviously been bleeding, as blood was showing in his urine. It was being monitored and I was told it was under control, but it was one more thing to worry about in what seemed like a never-ending list.

I was trying to cope with all the stress of the situation but the barrage of new information seemed to be unrelenting. There were the never-ending updates that just kept on coming and the results of all these different tests that would go back and forth on a constant basis. I knew the doctors were doing their best, but it seemed like they were changing their minds every five minutes as to what was the best way forward. It was overbearing and Mahmoud still remained in a critical condition. And that was just what was happening inside the hospital. Outside, I was having to deal with a different kind of pressure.

Every evening I would receive emails and messages from friends and family that I would have to respond to. My brothers, Shahram and Shahin, would send prayers and call me every day for an update. Of course I was incredibly grateful for their support but having to communicate with everyone along with all the travelling back and forth to the hospital each day was beginning to take its toll on me. I was exhausted.

I was also having many conversations across the world with my extended family, who all wanted to know how he was doing. One of those conversations was with my cousin Manijeh, who I was very close to and was a science lecturer at NYU. We would speak every night and with access to some of the latest medical research from the university, she would keep me updated on any developments that might affect the prognosis of Mahmoud's injuries. I also spoke to my cousin Minoo, one of the world's leading specialists in AIDS and infectious diseases and her husband, Koroush, a top surgeon. When I told them about what had happened with Mahmoud and his accident and then the severity of his subsequent injuries they began to call me regularly for news, whether it was a medical diagnosis update or just a progress report. I filled them in with as much information as I could and again it was good to be able to speak with people who had extensive medical knowledge but who were also family. It was during one of our conversations that they told me that I needed to prepare myself in case Mahmoud took a turn for the worse. Of course Minoo and Koroush were worried about him, but I realised that they were concerned for me as well and in the nicest possible way, were just being realistic. Being cruel to be kind you might say.

But I still believed in Mahmoud and the power of faith and its ability to heal. And then something happened that really scared me. One of the consultants, a New Zealander, was doing a test on Mahmoud when I arrived to see him. It wasn't easy to constantly keep on asking questions and the hospital staff did their best to keep us informed but I was relentless and wasn't going to leave any stone unturned if I thought it might help the situation. And on this occasion I wanted to know the answer to something in particular.

'Do you have any idea how long he is going to have to remain in intensive care?' I asked her.

'Well, in this country, under the NHS we will always continue to care for every patient,' she replied. As she was about to leave she turned and gave me a reassuring smile, 'Even if they only have a 7% chance of survival.'

She was actually trying to give me hope, but of course to hear that tiny percentage was devastating and hit me extremely hard. If I hadn't realised just how critical Mahmoud's condition was before, I certainly knew it now. I began to have some terrible thoughts. If the survival rate was so low, what if he did survive but came out not just physically impaired but mentally impaired too? Having had such an amazing and active life would poor Mahmoud be able to take it if he wasn't his normal self? Would I?

The consultant left and as I sat there and tried to process what I had just heard, emotion got the better of me and I cried. Reaching over to Mahmoud I took his hand in mine and held my Koran in the other. I leant in close to him.

'I'm sure you're not going to die Mahmoud, you're not going to die. You will survive,' I told him. I leant in even closer. 'I don't know if you can hear me, but if you can hear me, squeeze my hand.' His hands were difficult to hold because they had swollen by this point due to the trauma of his injuries and the fact that he wasn't really moving at all and so his circulation was very poor. His left thumb already had a nasty cut which had been stitched. To actually hold his hand you had to put your hand underneath his hand and gently hold his fingers. But he didn't respond to my question and there was no reaction. 'I just want to tell you that you're going to survive.' I was crying through my words as I spoke them but whether he could hear me or not, I had to give him hope.

The truth was that deep down, because of the severity of his injuries and because the doctors had kept on reminding us that he was not a young man, I didn't really know if I believed that he would make it. It was a low point and I realised that Mahmoud needed all the help he could get. Everybody had told me that when I sat with him that I had to give him energy. And so I got in touch with my cousin Mashid and as a Sufi, she responded by directing spiritual vibrations towards him. We arranged a time to speak at the hospital and when she called, I held the phone to Mahmoud's ear and Mashid sent him messages full of positivity and energy. I just hoped that by receiving this energy and hearing my words and prayers, it would help him to find the strength to survive. I was doing everything I could to help him and I would spend many moments just holding his hand as he lay there. As I did so, I wondered what he was actually going through.

An Education

I was still in the other world but I was now in the Kohinoor tandoori restaurant, surrounded by my Cambridge friends from the tavern restaurant the night before. I couldn't yet understand how I kept on arriving at these places. I was beginning to have a few concerns about a number of things but at least this was an old haunt from our Cambridge University days. It had become a regular dinner destination as a refuge from the dire food that was constantly served in our student halls. The name Kohinoor translates as the mountain of light and I wondered if that had any significance in any way.

I was still trying to find my feet in this unknown world and understand it all. But there was one thing that I did know for certain: it was great to be back on familiar territory once again. Being in the Kohinoor took me right back to Cambridge and I started to think about my time there and how I had managed to get to the university in the first place.

At school I was a scientist at heart and had wanted to pursue a degree in medicine or natural sciences. But Langley School had the worst science department in Norfolk. So I needed to find somewhere that matched my ambitions if I was to go to university. Aged seventeen, I decided to follow in my brother's footsteps and attended the Norwich Technical College to study for my zoology, botany and chemistry A-levels.

For the first time in my life I tasted real freedom. I wanted to live near the college, and after a bit of exploration found some local lodgings in Grove Rd, only about five hundred yards away from it. A terraced house with bedrooms on the first floor and dining room and kitchen on the ground floor, it seemed to be perfect. It was however undoubtedly a place with its own 'hidden charms' and it was not without its challenges.

One of them came in the form of the lovely landlady, Mrs Margetson. A woman of a certain age, she was very friendly and laid out the ground rules for the house upon my arrival…

'Just buy me a bottle of gin a month and you can do whatever you bloody hell like!' she exclaimed. So that's what I did. The situation suited me and I was able to concentrate my attention on my college studies as well as play as much as sport as I possibly could.

It appeared that everyone in Norwich seemed to know Mrs Margetson. She really was quite a character. Her hair was always in curlers and she used to serve up dinner with a cigarette in her mouth and on quite a few occasions ash would drop off the end of it and fall onto the food. This did not seem to faze her. 'Never mind darling, that's just nourishment!' she was fond of saying.

And the food definitely left a bit to be desired. Best described as British stodge it was a seemingly endless round of pies and semolina. Every night she used to pile it onto our plates. It certainly wasn't the tastiest food I had ever eaten but she was doing her best and hungry as I was, I ate it anyway.

Some of the 'hidden charms' were more interesting than others. Mrs Margetson had a daughter, Jill, a good-looking girl who lived in the house and worked locally. She was also very friendly but had her own unique way of showing it. I was lucky enough to be the beneficiary of quite a few late night visits as Jill matched my endeavours by pursuing her own particular kind of education…

With one bath to be shared between three lodgers our washing arrangements were also quite challenging, but I didn't mind it that much and just got on with it. But not everyone seemed able to do so. A young policeman, who had taken lodgings there at the same time as me, announced one day that he couldn't take it anymore and left.

I stayed on. I was actually quite fond of Mrs Margetson and her eccentric ways and the lodgings were so close to the college that it made my life very easy. Two years seemed to go past in a flash and having passed my A-levels, I was ready for the next part of my education.

***

I had applied to Durham University but a few years earlier my head had been turned when I had visited my cousin at Cambridge and attended one of their renowned college balls. I had been incredibly impressed by all the history and sporting romance that seemed to be embedded as part of the college's fabric and had truly thought it to be one of the most beautiful places that I had ever seen. And so, on a whim, I applied to get into Trinity, one of the most prestigious colleges in Cambridge. To my great surprise, I got a quick reply, inviting me for an interview.

The big day arrived and I travelled to Cambridge, excited but nervous as well. I had formed a plan. I was going to wow the interviewer with my achievements as captain of the (unbeaten) first XV rugby at Langley School, captain of tennis, schoolboy rugby player for the Eastern Counties, Victor Ludorum medals in athletics – I had a whole list with which to dazzle him.

I reached the interview room and after taking a deep breath, strode inside where, to my surprise, I was greeted by a profusion of stuffed and preserved insects of every kind imaginable. I knew that my interviewer, Mark Pryor, was a world-famous entomologist but it was still quite a shock. Recovering my composure, I introduced myself to him and the interview began. It proceeded well enough and as time went by I waited patiently for him to ask me all about my glittering sporting career. But he never did. All he could talk about was Iran and the famous Iranian poets. It went on and on until it seemed like we had covered every single detail about Iran and its history.

Whilst I was happy enough to do so I was also aware that my chances of getting into Cambridge appeared to be slipping away with every fast-disappearing minute. Finally, at the end of the interview he paused and looked me up and down as he considered his next topic of conversation. This was surely it. My moment to really shine and regale him with my exploits of sporting prowess.

'If I were you, I would apply to other universities,' he remarked.

'Okay, I'll do that,' I stammered.

I have to say that what I said internally to myself was not exactly the same as the response that I gave him, either in tone or use of language.

We shook hands and I left the interview dejected. I couldn't believe it. All that way for absolutely nothing. But on the way out I had an idea. I searched around a few corridors within the college until I finally found the ancient room that I was looking for. If I wasn't going to be studying at this great college then at least I could say that I had gone to the bathroom there and taken a pee in Trinity!

But I was really deflated. And angry too, not with my interviewer but with myself. I questioned my own audacity for applying in the first place. 'What made you do this? How dare you apply to the greatest college in Cambridge. What the hell were you thinking?' I continued to berate myself for quite a time as I sloped back to Norwich and my lodgings.

The next day I was lying in bed still feeling slightly sorry for myself when my landlady appeared at my door with a letter from Cambridge. Of course in those days your post often arrived the next day. I opened it fearing the worst and was astounded to read that I had been accepted. At first I thought that someone was playing a joke on me. I just couldn't believe it and read the letter over and over again until it began to sink in. My dream was now a reality and I was following great names like Newton, Darwin and Byron and going up to Trinity College, Cambridge.

I sent fifty pounds as caution money and then I went back to Iran for the summer where in a state of euphoria I became what you might call the 'cat's prick'! In my defence there were very few Oxbridge candidates in Iran at that time, so perhaps my behaviour can be slightly excused.

As it turned out, Mark Pryor became a great mentor to me. He taught me a great deal about life, academia and even my own country. Despite being the quintessential Englishman, he had also been born in Iran. He was an eminent zoologist as well as an entomologist, whilst his wife Sophie was the great-granddaughter of Charles Darwin. But perhaps the greatest benefit to me was that he was my personal tutor.

On one occasion, just before I took my finals, I went to his rooms for a one to one and a drink, as was the custom. But I wasn't quite feeling myself and it showed.

'Why do you look so miserable?' he asked.

'Because I am bloody scared of the exams,' I replied. I felt like an idiot standing in front of this great man, shaking like a leaf because I was worried about my exams.

'I think you're a very capable person, why are you so scared? All you want is a degree isn't it?'

'Yes. That's all I want.'

'Well, at Cambridge, at worst you can always get a special.' This was a lower-third degree and hardly worth having.

'But I don't think you should worry,' he continued, 'you're a very intelligent man you should have confidence in yourself. I've heard good reports about you. You should stop panicking and get a goodnight's sleep every night and don't worry about your exams. I can guarantee that you're going to pass.' He paused to let this information sink in. 'And now, all I want you to do is have a glass of sherry with me.'

Of course after that encouragement I was fine. His simple yet wise words gave me all the confidence I needed to get a good degree. He ended up having a profound influence on my life and on one occasion gave me some advice that I have never forgotten, 'In life always trust in yourself. Don't let your mind wander off to terrible things. Don't go into the abyss. Stay above it.'

I took this advice to heart and have practised it ever since. A few years later (after I had left Cambridge) he would also be involved in a bad car accident that would leave him in a vegetative state for three years before he eventually died. The world would lose a great man and his death would devastate me. He was to make a lasting impression on my life in more ways than one.

What are Friends for?

– *Prince Shabaz* –

I hate going to hospitals. I always get depressed when I visit and I know friends who, no matter who is in there, never set foot in them. But I didn't have a problem going to visit Mahmoud.

I had met him in the early eighties at Queen's before he married Sheida. We became friends because we shared a love for tennis. He was always indomitable on court and when he was running for the ball he would somehow always manage to get to it. I wasn't quite sure how he did that, but he never lacked in spirit. And Mahmoud was very easy to get along with. We got on very well because we both had been to school in England and knew what it was like to go through something like that. Getting a British education had helped him a great deal to deal with adversities in life and we saw eye to eye on a lot of things. So we understood each other Mahmoud and I.

One of the things that endeared Mahmoud to everyone was his complete lack of inhibition. He always said what was on his mind. You never had to pretend with him you were just who you were. Everyone loved Mahmoud for that reason and he was always able to make us laugh a lot. We got to know each other socially and we would see a lot of each other at parties. He was happiest going out for a curry and he would invite interesting people to join us and a good time was had by all.

When the accident happened I got a call from Sheida saying Mahmoud had been run over and that he was in critical condition in intensive care. So I found out exactly where he was and went to see him and of course was horrified with what greeted me. There was Mahmoud with all sorts of tubes sticking out of him and in a coma. He looked absolutely awful. I thought my God we can't lose Mahmoud he's too important to us all. None of us knew if he would make it because he had such trouble breathing. I kept wondering why they didn't operate but they have a policy of not doing anything when you are in a trauma like that because the body has ways of healing itself. At the time it didn't make much sense to me because I wanted them to just get on and fix him.

In one way I did feel bashful about going to see Mahmoud because if it was me and I wasn't well and I had people coming to see me I wouldn't want them to be there. I wouldn't want them to see me in such a weak, vulnerable situation. And there are a lot of people like that. You have to gauge when you should go and when you shouldn't go as some people just don't want you there. But on the other hand, I actually think one of the nicest things you can do for someone is to go and see them in hospital. Whenever someone you know is in hospital go and visit them as they will always remember it.

Quite frankly, when I saw him, I wasn't quite sure what to say to him. So I said, 'Mahmoud, what have you got yourself up to?' Or something like that. The problem was that I wasn't quite sure exactly what had happened. None of us really knew because none of us had been there. The doctors did not know either and were doing x-rays and MRIs to find out what was broken and what was intact.

I was just determined that he should get well. And I was going to be there to give him the support and energy to help him do that. I wanted him to know that we were there and that basically life was still worth living. But when he was in the coma he didn't respond in any way, he was totally out. That was very hard to bear because he could have been dead. The hospital stuff were fantastic they really were. So I knew I could only literally do so much for him and I wanted to help and support

Sheida because it couldn't have been easy for her. But again I wanted her to know that we were there for her and to give her courage. She was there all the time which was very hard for her.

The most difficult thing was not knowing what the outcome was going to be. The uncertainty was very difficult to live with. I also felt an incredible sense of frustration and not being able to do anything. That I found most difficult. I kept wanting the doctors to do this, that and the other, which was as much wanting to do just something to help him. I couldn't even bring him a cup of tea! So it was incredibly frustrating not being able to help directly.

As far as I was concerned he was going to make it if I had anything to do with it – which of course I didn't. But the worst thing of all was that deep down I really didn't know if my friend *was* going to make it. It was just terrible, the worst thing of all, not knowing. Giving up control was really hard. I always heard encouraging remarks from the doctors but I wasn't sure that anyone really knew what would happen. But it's funny how in the middle of a such a drama and despite all these major concerns, it's the little things that get to you. Day to day, one of the biggest issues was hoping that you would find a parking space! I used to dread going to the hospital because I would worry about where I was going to park.

What was so sad was that here was my great friend, renowned for his sense of humour and yet with the situation he was in nobody felt like cracking jokes. Sheida would talk quite normally to him whilst he was in a coma which helped bring some sense of normality to the situation.

But I knew that intrinsically Mahmoud had a great deal of optimism which is not something you can teach someone. It's part of who you are. You either have it or you don't. And he had it. Optimism coupled with a sense of humour.

So that's how it was. I went in to see him as often as I could, almost every day, because I wanted to make sure that the hospital was giving him the proper attention. It felt like the least I could do.

My Worst and Best Decision

It was so good to see my friends and it was just like old times. Even though it was in this strange other world, we were chatting, laughing and taking the rise out of each other. It was odd seeing them like this though. It wasn't so long ago that I had been thinking about what my life was like without them in it. We were all about the same age, enjoying our lives and then in a relatively short period of time one by one they had all gone, leaving me on my own. The impact of their deaths had had a huge effect on me. I felt like I had been abandoned. We were so close, had so much fun and had formed such a true bond of friendship. I still had the memories of our amazing experiences together, but their deaths had made me realise that we are all living on borrowed time. Anything could happen and it prepared me for my own mortality. Having known what those that had suffered with cancer had gone through in terms of chemotherapy, if I'm honest I had prayed that when my end did come that it would happen a little more quickly.

So I thought that part of my life had died with them and that was going to be that. But now here we were together once again. I wasn't sure what this really meant. I knew there had to be reason I was in this heavenly place and that I wanted to discover what I was doing here. But in this seemingly endless moment of time I was just happy they were there. And they did seem to be very content in this other world.

As we all enjoyed another meal together, I began to study them in a little more detail. In this world they all looked in extremely good condition. They were young, healthy versions of themselves. I smiled to myself as I made the observation because in this other world I too felt exactly the same way about myself. I hadn't actually looked in a mirror, but it was as much about how I felt and I felt young and energetic. It was as though we were all back in our twenties.

During that time we had always enjoyed meeting in restaurants whether it was Montpeliano's in London or here in the Kohinoor. I loved the atmosphere and bonhomie that one felt being in those kind of places. I had spent much of my working life sharing great moments with friends, work colleagues and clients in many restaurants across the world. But those great experiences were partly responsible for me making one of the worst decisions that I ever made. Conversely, it also led to one of the best moments in my life.

In the late nineties, after years of working in the corporate world it had dawned on me that there must be something else to do in life. I had been keeping my eye on the market for something new and exciting to emerge, when an opportunity arose. Through my sporting connections I had got to know a businessman – who I will refer to as Mr X – and one day he approached me saying that he had bought the lease on this property in a prime central London location. The proposition was to launch a restaurant selling newspapers and magazines to customers who could then read about what was going on in the world whilst they had something to eat. Believe it or not it seemed a fairly revolutionary idea at the time. And the particular words that Mr X used to sum up his pitch were unforgettable.

'Even if we serve shit, we should make millions,' he boldly stated.

At the time I had a business partner who wasn't known for throwing his money away and I went to him with the proposal. A very serious man, he agreed that it seemed to have great prospects as a flagship restaurant, with a lot of scope for further expansion and we decided to visit the property. It was only half-finished and hadn't yet been turned into a restaurant so I got my 'construction man' who had worked on my own property to have a look at it. He gave us a reasonable price and we agreed to go ahead with the investment in the project. For a small, initial capital outlay, we would have a 49% stake in the business and Mr X and his partners would retain a 51% share.

After three months of hard work the restaurant was finally finished. We opened and immediately created a bit of a buzz in the local area. I was very much hands on and put my heart and soul into the venture. At first it seemed as though the business was doing really well. The restaurant was packed out each day and our reputation appeared to be growing. But then I discovered that there were things going on behind the scenes that were out of my control.

Our partner Mr X appeared to be virtually illiterate in terms of business sense and really had no idea of what to do. His mother, who was a prominent figure on the other side of the partnership, had, unbeknownst to us, actually been the person who had purchased the lease on the building and had subsequently voted him out of the business, retaining the majority shareholding. Getting rid of Mr X should have given us an opportunity to consolidate the business and take it forward. But the mother had other ideas. She had another son who she favoured and wanted him to become involved with the business. This presented us with an even bigger problem. The other son was even more useless than his brother.

The first time we really knew what was happening was when he began to turn up at the restaurant. He would arrive with his Alsatian dog and, always short of money, would literally put his hand in the till, grab a handful of cash and leave an IOU instead. Despite our protestations this would occur on a daily basis. And we were powerless to stop it. Soon after, the arguments with his mother started and he would fight with her and later on with his brother as well. To the outside world, everything seemed to be going well. We were working hard and the restaurant was busy for lunch and dinner every day. In reality, we didn't know where the money was disappearing to. It was a nightmare. But as minority shareholders our hands were tied and we couldn't do anything about it. In the meantime we had both continued to invest more funds into the business, convinced that things would soon turn around. But instead of getting better, the financial situation got even worse. Rather than getting back on an even keel, we proceeded to lose even more money. The whole thing was a fiasco and eventually I decided that enough was enough and pulled out of the venture early. The reality of running one successful restaurant was well and truly over, let alone any dream of opening a chain of them across London. I had tried to do something different in life, but in the end it hadn't worked out the way that I had planned it. The restaurant had been a great idea, but the operation was hopeless and I incurred a huge financial loss. My business partner stayed in even longer than I did and sadly lost even more money. However, amongst all the gloom and doom there was one ray of sunshine.

A year into the business, on one particular day I walked into the restaurant and I saw this beautiful woman, dressed immaculately and with an incredible sense of style. She was sitting at one of the tables and with her was a striking-looking girl who looked around twenty years old. The beautiful woman possessed a European look that was understated and incredibly elegant. I was transfixed by her and I asked Mr X if he knew who she was. He told me that she was an Iranian lady who was there with her daughter. I hadn't even realised that she could be Iranian because of her European look. He then told me that he had actually met them before and I immediately asked him for an introduction. He duly made one and we began talking. I couldn't take my eyes off this beautiful woman and she seemed to be showing a similar interest in me. It was love at first sight. I discovered that she played tennis and so I invited her to play at Queen's. We became playing partners and soon afterwards our friendship blossomed into a romance. Of course the beautiful woman with the stylish look and amazing grace was Sheida.

I came back into the moment in the other world. My friends were still around me and we were still having a great time, but my memory of Sheida and her daughter, Samira, had got me thinking. Something else was now happening. Different emotions were stirring inside me and I was beginning to feel a bit more unsure about my situation. I was surrounded by friends, yes, but I was also was missing the other people in my life. I was missing those that those I was closest to. I loved this other world, with all its beauty, tranquillity and sense of peace, but now there was something that was really bothering me. If I was up here with no-one else apart from my friends, where was everyone else? Where was Sheida?

What Happens Next?

– Sheida –

I was in the hospital sitting by Mahmoud's side. Progress seemed painfully slow and I still didn't know yet whether Mahmoud was going to have any of the operations or not. What I did know was that Mahmoud was here and that I was with him. And with so many problems still to be resolved, coupled with the stress of the whole situation, any little moments of comfort were most welcome.

One of them came in the form of an Iranian orthopaedic surgeon, Mr Hamid Reza Haj Hassany. He was the head of orthopaedics at St Mary's. When he had seen the name Mahmoud Izadi as one of the patients who needed orthopaedic care, he recognised the Iranian name and had made a note to come to see him. Of course by the time he arrived, Mahmoud was already in an induced coma and so couldn't speak to him. But I chatted with him and I found a small sense of relief in having a little bit of familiarity amongst all the uncertainty that was going on.

By now I had entered into a familiar routine with Mahmoud. I would sit with him, hold his hand and either talk or continue to use my Koran to try and help heal his other injuries. In the ICU there were three other beds available for others who, like Mahmoud, had sustained serious trauma and had been involved in other road traffic accidents. A constant flow of various other patients were brought in and out and one day a young boy came in who had been on a motorbike and had been hit by a bus. He wasn't in a very good way and looked to have some very severe injuries. His family came in to visit him and they were naturally upset to see him in such an unfortunate state. It was very sad to see and I wished him and them well.

The next day I had been sitting with Mahmoud for a few hours when I decided that I needed to have a break. I spent as much time as possible with him but it was very draining, both mentally and physically being in the ICU for such long periods. I went and checked with one of the nurses to see if there had been any more updates and then made my way to the waiting room that was adjoined to the ICU. I sat down and took a few deep breaths. It was good just to get away from everything even if it was only for a short while. Through the doorway, the rush of hospital life continued in front of me, as various consultants, specialists and nurses hurried back and forth in and out of the ICU.

My mind had drifted off when a slight commotion through the doorway caught my attention. Intrigued, I looked up to see what the cause of it was. A large trolley came into view as it was being wheeled past the doorway. I had seen plenty of trolleys in the hospital but there was something slightly different about this one. On it was something encased in purple plastic and at first I wasn't sure what it was. But then to my horror I realised what was happening. They were removing the body of the young motorcyclist from the ICU. He clearly hadn't made it. It sent a shiver down my spine. I took a breath and tried to regain my composure. The poor boy had been so young and I thought about the tragic loss of life and what his family must be going through. It brought everything that much closer to home. Of course this was the harsh reality of somewhere like the ICU but it was harrowing all the same. It really shook me up and I thought about Mahmoud and wondered whether he would ever come out of the coma. But I was determined to keep positive and keep believing.

My days were now getting later and I would get home at 9:30 pm and then deal with all the emails or phone calls with family members, many of whom who were operating on different time zones as they were calling from across the States. Part of the stress of dealing with all the communications was because of the kind of story that I was having to recount. Mahmoud had received a miracle concerning his ribs and that had helped with the fluid in the lung problem, for now at least. But the truth was that he was a seventy-eight-year-old man who was severely injured, the consultants were considering up to four major operations on his spine, brain, hip and knee and he was in an induced coma just to keep him alive. No matter how positive I was, and no matter the best thoughts and wishes of all our friends and family, I was having to retell a story many times to lots of different people where in all probability the outcome was that Mahmoud was not going to survive. To make matters worse, I had no appetite and so was hardly eating anything and was also having trouble sleeping. I wasn't about to give up on Mahmoud, far from it, but it was incredibly hard to keep going day after day and I honestly wasn't sure how long I could go on for. I decided that I had to have a break and went to stay with my daughter and grandchildren in Ealing. They were incredibly kind to me and it was wonderful to have a change in environment and be looked after for a while. But I still went in to the hospital every day to see Mahmoud.

And then news came through that the consultants had made a decision about his spine operation. It was a week after his spine had been crushed in the accident and with the pressure now released on his lungs they wanted to proceed with the operation. And so they went ahead with it. It was incredibly stressful waiting for the outcome of the operation. Time seemed to stand still but eventually after four hours it was over. The surgeon informed us that it had been successful and the relief was incredible.

Mahmoud was now transferred to a private room in the ICU because of risk of infection. This was another step into the unknown. By the door of the private room there were a selection of surgical masks and gloves which any visitor who entered the room could wear to help prevent the spread of any germs. Mahmoud was allowed to have two visitors in the private room at any one time and he was attended by a nurse on twenty-four supervision. The first time that I entered the room she assured me that everything was 100% sterilised but I insisted on wearing both a mask and gloves because I didn't want him to pick up any infection. When Nilu visited she also wore a mask as she wanted to kiss her father on his face. Everything *was* clean and perfect in the room but we didn't want to take any chances. Visitors were also asked to undertake the same protocol. If the visitor slots were already full, new visitors would wait in the waiting room until a slot became available. The two visitor slots were very rarely free.

To aid his recovery post operation, he was given a fluid mixture of banana and milk to help his body to absorb calcium and to help prevent any damage to his bones. It was a small detail but it seemed like a positive step in the right direction. But although the operation had seemingly gone well, Mahmoud was still in the induced coma and I felt extremely uncomfortable not being able to talk to him after such a major event. The private room was a different environment, but I soon continued my routine of watching, waiting and praying. I wondered what further challenges we were going to have to face and what would happen next.

My Family

I was with my friends once more in this heavenly place. Foulad and I had separated from the others and he turned round to me and gave me one of his best smiles.

'Am I going to beat you again today?' he said.

'No, not this time,' I replied. I knew exactly what he was talking about. It was how we had first met at Cambridge. I had arrived at Trinity College and the euphoria I had felt at having got a place there had been replaced by a feeling of being overwhelmed by all the other students. They were all wearing gowns and as they hurried back and forth from their lectures and society meetings, looked completely at home in their surroundings. Some of them were the worst public school types who were very ostentatious and didn't really look at me or give me the time of day. I thought it was because I was a foreigner. I was certainly an outsider as there had only ever been three other Iranians at Trinity before me. Some of the other British students did appear to have a less insular outlook on life and I made friends with a few of them. But the whole place felt like another world and I needed to find a way to make my mark. As had happened previously in my life, it was through sport that I managed to do so.

It was summer and I had turned my attention to tennis. I became friends with Parviz Radji who wanted to introduce me to a friend of his by the way of the fact that he had laid a wager that I could beat him at tennis. I fancied my chances and thought that I could beat anybody from the Middle East, so

I accepted the wager. We played, but he was a brilliant player and just too good for me. And that was how I had met Foulad.

We went on to become best friends and share many adventures together. He was part of an established set that had all been to Victoria College in Alexandria. Through Foulad I met the others including Piero, Janeau, Ghassan and Maan. Although they were well established as a group of friends, they welcomed me into the fold and we quickly became brothers in arms.

My friendship with Foulad was cemented one day when he challenged me to a race to the pub. He was driving a Ford Consul and I had my Triumph TR2. We were to race to a restaurant in St Neots just outside Cambridge. We set off down the country roads, with him taking the lead and before long I decided that it was my turn to take over at the front. But as soon as I drove up to overtake him he would swerve over to the middle of the road making it impossible for me to pass. I pulled back and tried again on the other side but the same thing happened. This sparring went on for several miles, but try as I might I just couldn't find a way past him. I decided that enough was enough and chose to pull back a little bit. It was at this exact point that a police car appeared from a speed trap that had set up ahead and pulled us both over. They had been waiting to spring their trap and as they took down our details one of the policemen addressed me.

'You're a sensible chap because you didn't try to overtake him when he wouldn't let you,' he said in his broad local dialect. 'But you did nearly run over that cyclist. He's in the ditch over there and for all I know he might be dead.' We all turned round to see that a cyclist was indeed sprawled in a ditch. We rushed over to check whether he was okay but luckily he wasn't injured and was just a bit shaken up. Somehow I managed to get away from the incident scot-free, but Foulad had to go to court and ended up losing his licence for six months. Despite this outcome, the experience helped form an unbreakable bond between the two of us and we became friends for life.

And now here I was about to play tennis with him again in this other world. We were at a tennis court in Thompson's Lane in Cambridge, where we had played all those years before. It was very strange but at the same time perfectly normal. We started playing tennis but there was something odd about the game. I couldn't put my finger on what it was and we were still hitting the ball back and forth to each other, but it didn't feel quite right. I had noticed that this was a common theme in this world. It was difficult to ascertain exactly what was wrong but it was as if you couldn't quite feel the touch of things.

We continued playing, both of us joking with one another and each of us trying to get an edge. But then straight after the game the same thing happened as before. Without really being aware of how it had happened, suddenly I was back in my house again. It was now becoming the norm, but it still took some getting used to. Looking around my space I noticed my desk in the corner and decided it was a good place to go and take stock and try and makes some sense of what was happening.

Although in this other world I was with my friends I wasn't actually *with* them. It was like I was in some way removed from the present. On the one hand I was healthy, I was relaxed and I was happy. But on the other, I also felt apprehensive. I was fulfilled but my mind was getting disturbed. And I was beginning to feel a little isolated because I couldn't control anything. I had no way of contacting anyone, not even my old friends. Each time that I wanted to see them, I had to wait for them just to appear. This heavenly place was indeed a paradise, but up here, I was alone.

My cousin Nasser had met me and introduced me to this other world but the last thing I knew was that he was alive and well and living a fantastic life between the South of France and London. What was he doing here? I didn't know where Sheida and Nilu were, but I was absolutely sure they weren't with me in this world. And what about my Cambridge friends? If they were here why weren't any members of my family here? Where were my uncles and aunts and grandparents? There were quite a lot of them and they had a pretty interesting history.

***

My great grandfather Naser-din Shah Qajar was the longest ruling monarch in Iran and ruled for forty-nine years before he was assassinated whilst he was praying in a shrine in 1895. His assassin objected to him giving the tobacco concession to the British, so he killed him. He had a daughter who was my grandmother, Ezat Saltaneh, she lived to the age of ninety-five and died in 1986. She married a Qajar prince, the son of one of the Shah's brothers Ehtesham el Molk – Ehtesham of the land – a very wealthy landowner. He owned Daroos and estates in the north of Tehran. My grandmother and grandfather had four daughters and two sons. One of them was my mother, Monir-eaghdas. Neither she nor her brothers were in line to the throne.

At Cambridge, I had been very keen to see Trinity College's renowned Wren Library. A masterpiece of architecture designed by the famous architect Sir Christopher Wren, I had been fascinated by it from afar and was even more amazed at what I found inside when I finally got there. Amongst the comprehensive book collections I discovered a large selection of books on Iran. In this pre-internet age this was fairly illuminating in itself, but there was even more to come. Some of the books contained comprehensive details about my forefathers of the Qajar dynasty and I saw pictures of my uncles in the books which was an incredible feeling. It inspired me and made me very proud to have achieved a place there.

My grandfather had owned 300,000 square metres of land in Daroos by the foot of the mountains where we all lived. When he died he split his land between his children but Muslim law favoured the sons with a greater possession – the sons getting two-thirds and daughters getting one-third each. As a child I remembered learning that the land was agricultural, farmed by Rayaat, the labourers of the land. A mixture of oxen tilling the land, orchards and farmland, in today's values it would now be worth over a billion pounds.

In 1928, my family, the Qajars, were overthrown by the Pahlavi dynasty. Reza Shah was a powerful man, a true patriot who rose up through the army ranks and replaced a young Qajar Shah who was spending a lot of his time in Paris. The young Shah was forced to abdicate but it was no bad thing as he was too inexperienced and preferred his roulette tables in the West. It was Reza Shah's son, Mohammad Reza Shah, who would make a decision that would have a huge impact on my life.

At Cambridge I had realised that one of the greatest services that I could give my family was to become the estate agent of my grandfather's land in the north. This would be a role that I created for myself. The land operated under a feudal system and with my estate management background from my Cambridge studies, I had a vision of how the running of the land could be modernised and brought up speed. I believed that this would benefit everyone including those operating and working on the land.

I graduated from Cambridge and was working as a trainee for Fisons in Ipswich, England. Amongst other products, the company made chemical fertilisers and I wanted to get some knowledge of modern agricultural methods. After a year working for them I had learnt a great deal but had a sense of responsibility to go back to my country. The estate land had a vast amount of scope and was suitable for either arable or dairy farming. The seasonal weather in the Caspian was fantastic and the potential seemed to be unlimited. My vision was to introduce commercial agriculture methods for the land and I planned on spending six months visiting and assessing different options for each area. Nothing had changed in thousands of years and it was going to be the first ever instance of such methods in Iran. I was on cloud nine as I laid out my plans. This was an opportunity to bring farming in Iran into the twentieth century and beyond.

But then something extraordinary happened. Without warning, the Shah introduced the first of a series of land reform bills. They would have deep ramifications both for the country and myself. Firstly, it meant the demise of the existing feudal system which, whilst it badly needed the modernisation I could bring to it, as a system actually worked perfectly well. Secondly, and more importantly as far as my immediate future was concerned, the new nationalisation meant that our family would lose all our land. It was devastating and hurtful. The clergy did challenge the ruling and among their number was a young cleric who had ambitions of his own. Ayatollah Khomeini would make his own mark years later, rising to power and overthrowing the Pahlavi dynasty ending 2,500 years of continuous rule by the Persian monarchy in the Iranian revolution of 1979. But the Shah did not care about the clergy and dismissed their claims.

Despite a strong opposition – Iran was known as the country of a thousand families – nobody had any power to oppose the Shah and the land reforms were passed through parliament. My dreams of land management were over and my life would take a completely different turn.

***

Back in the other world, I wondered what I should do next. The scenario here never changed, it was almost like a suspended world with its constant peace and tranquillity. I couldn't believe how beautiful it all was and I didn't feel under any pressure – none of the day to day stuff that I normally had to deal with was apparent. No bills, bad news, deaths or tragedies. But I was beginning to have *some* queries about this paradise. It was slightly eerie that there were no gatherings or parties. And the restaurants were packed with people but I didn't know any of them. But the biggest query that I had concerned my parents. Where were they? Why could I not find them in this heavenly place?

My earliest memory of my mother was as a very small boy. I was in her arms as she was getting ready to attend one of her royal family's many huge gatherings. She was dressed up to the nines wearing a stunning red and white dress set off by brooches and a pearl necklace. On her hand was this incredible diamond-studded sapphire ring – which my sister, Lili, now wears today. My mother was trying to hand me over to the nanny and I wasn't too happy about it and I was screaming and crying because I didn't want her to leave.

But despite that memory, I had a superb relationship with my mother. She actually always put my brother Masoud and myself before anything else in her life. She attended us, looked after us and always tried to give us the best food. She loved my brother, my sister and myself equally, although my sister always thought that she favoured her sons. But my brother and I were the ones that were sent away to boarding school as children. It had a profound effect on me when it came to relationships. When a girl left me I became traumatic. I had it happen three times in my life with three girls that I loved. They all left me, probably because I didn't treat them that well, but I didn't expect them to leave me! This feeling of rejection also transferred to friendships as well. Whenever I had a fallout, however temporary, it had the same effect on me and I hated it because of the rejection. But I didn't hold any of this against my mother. She was the most loving, generous and funny woman and as the granddaughter of the Shah, a true princess. My brother and I were her children and she never fully acknowledged us as grown-ups until the day that she died.

My father, Hasan Izadi, came across as a very harsh man and my mother used to try and protect us from him. In Iran in those days to assert your authority you used to beat your children. He never actually made contact with me, but he used to raise his hand as a threat and that was enough to scare the life out of me. When we were young boys my brother and I would come back from the local school and we would run riot in the house. But we were always afraid of my father and as soon as he arrived home we became like a couple of mice and behaved ourselves. Unlike my mother, my father never displayed his emotions. He never cuddled us or kissed us as children. It was only when he got older and I was looking after him that he would show signs of affection. We did have our moments together however.

When Khomeini came to power there were riots and a feeling of lawlessness in the streets. In Tehran my father had two hotels, the Marmar and the Sorya. I didn't work in the hotels as such, but as a result of my time spent living in England I thought that I had seen a gap in the market for an idea involving one of them. I decided to approach my father with it.

'What if we opened the first English pub in Iran inside the Marmar?' I suggested.

'What, you mean like the pubs that we drink in when we're in London?' he replied, clearly surprised by the idea.

'Exactly,' I said, pleased he was even considering it.

'Why not?' he said. And then added, 'but you would have to organise and design the whole thing.'

My first challenge was to create the blueprint for the pub. The hotel already had a huge bar that aside from the odd client or guest lay empty for most of the time. With very happy memories of my times spent in pubs in my Cambridge days, playing rugby and as part of my social life in London, I had plenty of inspiration and ideas to draw from. I decided to keep everything very simple. I named the new venture 'The Pub' and built the pub interior around the existing bar in the hotel.

The next challenge was to create the feel of an authentic English pub. I decided to offer an English breakfast to remind English customers of a taste of home. But I wanted something more, something which was both quintessentially English and encouraged a greater social element. I decided that having a dartboard was the answer. You couldn't buy those in Tehran but I found a source in the UK, although I was reprimanded on several occasions by a cousin who worked in Customs and Excise for bringing 'sharp' arrow-like darts into the country.

The biggest difficulty I had was getting hold of beer that I could serve in the pub. I wanted to serve English beer, but the very first keg I managed to get hold of was actually from Carlsberg, organised by a friend of mine. After three months of hard work everything was in place and we opened for business. I had managed to get word out about this exciting new addition to Tehran's social scene and its popularity grew quite quickly. Before long it became the central meeting point for all the English mechanics and engineers who were based in Tehran. Things were going well, but I had a problem. The importation process to get the Carlsberg beer into Iran was complicated and dealing with all the red tape was taking far too long. It was a complete nightmare and I knew that I needed to find another solution for buying the beer and find it pretty fast.

The issue I had was that even if I found an English beer to import, I would still run into the same issues with the local customs. But The Pub had clearly made an impact and news of what I was doing had reached some unlikely ears. I was approached by an Iranian beer manufacturer. They suggested that I use their own local beer instead of going through the hassle of all the importation. I was a bit sceptical as I was used to English or European beer – how good could this local beer really be? But taking the attitude of nothing ventured nothing gained, I decided to give it a go. I was pleasantly surprised by the taste. It was fantastic! If anything it was better than the beer that I was used to drinking. From that point onwards our pub only served Iranian Shams beer. It had a high alcohol content and seemed to go down very well with the customers.

The Pub went from strength to strength and the darts really took off with various matches and even a darts league. Word began to spread even further afield and customers started coming from all over Iran and we started serving other foreign nationals working in Iran including Dutch and German workers. My father couldn't believe how well it was doing. We had effectively opened Iran's first ever pub! It was a great moment for both of us. Later on, when the new rulers of the regime took over my father's hotel after the revolution, the reason that they gave for doing so was that alcohol was being sold there. But of course by then, every hotel in Tehran was selling alcohol. Perhaps they were just jealous of the success of our little venture.

***

My mother's death in 1993 had a profound effect on me and it took me almost three years before I got over it. She had suffered a stroke three years previously and I had tended to her during that time. She lived next door to me in London and I was available to her virtually twenty-fours a day. She would miss me and then that would turn into a panic attack. It meant that I never had a holiday during this period, but that didn't matter to me because I wasn't just caring her for in the physical sense. I loved her with all my heart and my soul.

When she died, she was laid to rest in the hospital chapel and my brother and I went to see her and pay our respects. It was the first time in my life that I had seen a dead body. Since having her stroke she had always suffered. She had worn this grimace on her face, which had given her a constant pained expression. But looking at her in that moment, all the pain and anguish had vanished and she looked totally at peace. In fact I had never seen such peace in my life. She was such a faith-orientated woman and my belief in her faith for her went sky high. I carefully cut off a lock of her hair for a keepsake. She was buried at Hampstead cemetery at Fortune Green and I used to go and visit her once a week. I needed that connection with her. She was at rest but you could say that I wasn't. Her grave was under a beautiful tree and I used go there to pray, cry and grieve.

Thinking these thoughts made me even more determined than ever to find my parents. It felt like my childhood past was repeating itself in this other world and I wanted to have them back in my life. I just wanted to see them again.

Quite A Character
– *Mehrdad* –

I visited Mahmoud most days in hospital because of the affection I have for him. I first met him when we were neighbours back in the mid-sixties in Kensington, London. In fact as it turns out, our families go back way further than that as Mahmoud's family home in Tehran was immediately opposite ours, although I didn't know him back then. As was the case with a lot of Mahmoud's friends, it was at Queen's that I really got to know him.

Whenever I saw Mahmoud he was always so positive. He always maintained that he was fine and was doing well. He had this optimistic approach to things and I never heard him in the worst of circumstances complain about anything. Such was his positivity that one day I joked with him about the different approaches to life.

'What's the difference between an optimist and a pessimist?' I said.

'I don't know,' he replied.

'A pessimist is someone who thinks that things cannot get worse, whereas an optimist is someone who thinks that they can.'

I'm a political activist and do a lot of media work but my time is my own and I tried to understand what was happening to Mahmoud. Our world has become so much smaller because you don't have that many friends that you have bonded with around you anymore. And Mahmoud is a very decent individual and a very good friend. I didn't perhaps subconsciously realise how I felt until this happened. In life, there are times when you feel as a friend that you have to be supportive and show up. I'm old-fashioned in standards and I felt that I had to do a bit extra. Those kind of things are important to me and it was not a chore to do so.

The key to our friendship has always been having mutual friends and mutual social interests. For example we both love curries. I have been going to a favourite Nepalese restaurant, Munal Tandoori, on the Upper Richmond Rd, for about twenty-five years. On one occasion I decided to take Mahmoud there for a meal. We had a fantastic evening and he loved it. Subsequently, I was away on business when Mahmoud remembered the restaurant and decided to take his brother and family there by themselves. But he had chosen a Friday night which can be extremely busy and with the rush of people coming and going, unfortunately the service wasn't up to the usual standard. Mahmoud wasn't having a great time as a result and started complaining to the owner and telling him that he wasn't at all impressed. The owner of the restaurant used to work at the Nepalese embassy in Tehran and so spoke a little Farsi and was certainly left in no doubt about what Mahmoud thought about the evening. When I returned to London, I met up with Mahmoud and he let rip about the whole experience and let me know in no uncertain terms what a dreadful evening it had been, how disgraceful the whole thing was, how let down he felt and how he would never step foot in the place again.

Anyway, after two or three months had passed I wondered whether Mahmoud might have calmed down about the whole thing. I thought I would test the waters and told Mahmoud that I was going there for a meal with my wife and asked him if he would like to accompany us. To my surprise he agreed. When we arrived I thought that I should clear the air and I called the owner over. I explained that here was this great friend of mine who was very disappointed with him and his restaurant staff as he had come here with his family for a great meal only to be embarrassed in front of them by the poor service. I then proceeded to tell the owner that I had gone to great lengths to persuade Mahmoud to come back and give them another chance and how I was sure that they would be incredibly grateful to have his custom. The owner waited patiently whilst I told my story and then when I had finished he graciously smiled at me, took one look at Mahmoud and simply said, 'He's been back since.' Mahmoud just exploded with laughter.

And that is Mahmoud all over. An extremely kind individual who bears no malice against anyone and is a non-confrontational and non-conflict seeking kind of person. He shies away from any kind of tension or dire situation by instinct. He does not want to get involved in any kind of arrangement that is upsetting for him. He tries to keep away from situations of that nature. Not that he does that all the time, but some people are not adversely affected by having to confront people. But Mahmoud naturally does not want to do that. You know that there is no hidden agenda with him and he is a very honest man. Because of that I have never had any kind of problems. I knew of his business associates but our relationship was purely social.

Of course I was concerned about what he was going through and so I called my brother who is a surgeon, explaining what had happened to Mahmoud. He asked me what his symptoms were and how old he was. When I told him, he informed me that his prospects were not that great and that he might not make it. The gravity of the situation became apparent then. But I knew that because of his sporting prowess, Mahmoud's body was strong and that despite everything he was physically in good shape for a man of his age. I also knew that if anyone stood a chance of coming through something like this, it was Mahmoud.

I Love You Daddy

Wanting to find my own parents led me to thinking about the fact that I was also a parent. I thought of my daughter Nilu and wondered where she was and what she was doing. I would never forget the dramatic circumstances in which she was born. I was in Israel on business when I received a phone call from my mother-in-law. We had never had the easiest of relationships so for her to call me like this meant it had to be important news.

'Darling, your wife is in the hospital, she is bleeding heavily, you have probably lost your child, but your wife may survive,' she exclaimed.

I was on the next plane back to London. Kukuly, my first wife, had indeed haemorrhaged and had been rushed into hospital. Nilu was born three weeks early and put into an incubator but miraculously survived. The circumstances had been exaggerated in the phone call but it was obviously serious enough. However, the outcome was the best one that I could have hoped for and I was now a father to a lovely, baby girl.

My first marriage had never been particularly easy because in truth, we weren't particularly well suited. We had met because I had happened to be sitting next to Kukuly's mother having been invited to a British embassy dinner in Tehran. She was a prominent society figure and was married to the first Iranian to head up the Iranian Oil Company and who would later go on to even bigger things and help in the formation of OPEC. We had talked at the dinner and the next day she had contacted me and arranged an introduction to her daughter. We both then met and embarked on a whirlwind romance and within six weeks we were married! She had a two-year-old daughter, Christina from a previous marriage who I raised as my own. She called me Dad and I put her through Heathfield school. Then Nilu was born six years later in 1971. Years later when I bought a racehorse, I named her Nilustina, combining my daughter's and stepdaughter's two names.

After Nilu's birth, her mother needed to recuperate from her difficult pregnancy and went back to Iran to do so. This presented me with a difficult dilemma because I obviously wanted the best for Nilu but at the time I was flat out working all hours in the oil industry. I decided the best thing to do was enrol her into the best nursery I could find, which in those days was in Hungerford, Berkshire. It wasn't a perfect scenario by any imagination, but I made sure that I could go and visit her every weekend. But after a while I couldn't take it anymore and one day I decided enough was enough. I engaged the services of a nanny who had looked after Nilu at the nursery and I phoned my wife in Tehran and told her that I had brought Nilu home. Luckily, the nanny had completely fallen in love with her which made the transition a whole lot easier.

My wife and I decided to make a go of things and we moved back to Iran to live there. Her father bought us a beautiful house to live in but it was all to no avail and we couldn't make things work between us. I decided to leave her but only on the condition that I would never lose touch with Nilu. They came back to London and we agreed that Nilu would stay with her mother. Despite relations between Nilu's mother and myself not being particularly cordial, I managed to take Nilu regularly to nursery each day. She then went on to the Hampshire School, on to Heathfield to complete her school education before studying at University in America and finally Farnham Art School.

During this whole time one incident stood out in particular. Nilu's mother and her family had properties all around the world and on one occasion I went to visit Nilu when she was with her mother in their apartment in Rome. When I arrived I was invited inside to find Nilu, four years old, sitting by the door waiting for me. In that moment I knew that whatever was said or suggested by others, no amount of money or influence could break the bond between me and my daughter.

***

Back in the other world, I needed to try and do something to find some answers to the questions I had. I didn't know how to get in touch with anyone and so I decided to see what else was outside the confines of my garden and see what I could find. I started exploring the area and soon found that my grandmother's house was nearby. My cousin's house was also very near me and my parents' house was about half a mile away. And my grandfather's house was north of where I lived. It was extraordinary. I knew that in the world that I had come from that none of these houses existed anymore. They had all been converted into high rises. But in my transcendence they were all here as though nothing had ever happened. I visited each one in turn and when I got to each house I just stood outside them. They were totally empty with no sign of life in any of them. I couldn't understand it. Where was everyone in this world? There didn't seem to be anyone around at all.

But visiting these houses from my life had a deep effect on me and all these childhood memories now came flooding back. Every year the Nowruz, meaning the new day, on March 20th, heralded the start of spring. And from that day forwards, the weather became like a paradise: warm, sunny and with the temperature rising up each day. We would live outside during this time. And once we were old enough we would go and play football. We would find some wasteland and just kick a ball around for hour after hour. At that age it seemed like a simple, never-ending pleasure.

My mother used to take me to the bazaar when I was a young boy and I was in heaven as I explored all the carts laden with sprawling fruits such as melons, grapes and quinces with the scent of cinnamon filling the air. The feasts at my grandfather's estate were also spectacular. My favourite dishes as a child were beautiful Persian rice dishes such as Loobia Polo with meat, French beans, rice and a whole host of exotic spices. I loved Estamboli Polo with tomato and rice and then Tahchin. But then I loved all the food including aubergine stews, vegetable stews and Chelo kebabs. There were would be huge family gatherings and parties where tables would be laden with this incredible array of food.

My brother and I attended the local Ferdowsi school, named after one of Iran's greatest poets who wrote the *Shahnameh* (Book of Kings). During the Islamic invasion of Iran, Arabs had tried to destroy our language by burning all the books and so the poet was paid by the king at the time to write poetry and verse in Persian to maintain the language. All the students in the school would gather every day to sing the Iranian national anthem every day before going to our classes.

Mount Damavand is the most beautiful mountain in Iran and has a snow-capped peak the whole year round. It is north of Tehran and as a boy growing up I would use it as my compass. Whenever I could see it I would know where I was. It was a visually magnificent spectacle. And there were other assaults on my senses as well. My mother was a great horticulturist and she grew amazing roses. In the Middle East roses have an incredibly strong aroma and when I used to come back home in the evenings the scent would be intoxicating and would blanket the whole garden with this incredible perfume.

The Shah's father had built the Pahlavi Avenue, which was the most beautiful tree-lined avenue in Tehran. In the south of the city all the political buildings, the ministry of foreign affairs and the parliament were decorated in stunning mosaics. These were the landmarks of my youth and I was lucky to enough to appreciate their beauty. All these memories made me very nostalgic. Thinking about my world growing up made me think about all the people that were in it. And somehow I decided that this was the moment I had been waiting for. I was going to find out where my parents were.

I calmly went back to my house and sure enough before long, I transcended once more and was back with my friends. I wasn't exactly getting used to this transcendence but I had accepted that in this other world this was how things worked. I was back in the Kohinoor but with my other friends engaged in conversation I managed to get Foulad's attention and draw him to one side. He seemed pleased to see me as usual, but now I needed his help and had some serious questions for him. I felt that he was open to having a conversation and that he seemed to sense that I was struggling with an issue.

'I need to speak to you,' I said. 'I've got something that's on my mind. It's really bothering me and I need to discuss it with you.'

'What is it?' he asked.

'I can't understand why I can't find my parents.' I said. The whole time that I had been with my friends in this other world we had discussed many things, but we had never talked about death. Neither theirs nor mine if indeed that is what had happened to me. But the subject was implicit in my question. Foulad didn't seem to be shocked by it and it was almost as if he was expecting it.

'Mahmoud they're here. They see you every day,' he replied.

'Yes, but where are they?' I remarked.

'They're here, but you can't see them because you're not supposed to be here.'

'But I am here,' I said, finding his comment a strange thing to say.

'To us you're here, but not to them.'

Foulad gave me a reassuring smile but before I could ask him anything else I found myself transcended back to my house. Was that it? Was that the only answer I was going to get? What did he mean by his words? We're happy to see you but you can't see them? I just didn't understand what it all meant. If I wasn't meant to be there where was I meant to be?

This was heaven. My personal heaven. It was what I saw and perceived and loved. There wasn't a thing that irritated me or took me away from peace and calmness. All the time that I was up there, even though I was missing Sheida and my daughter Nilu, I felt so strong and I wasn't afraid. At the same time I was wondering what I was doing in such a place. Despite all the apprehension and isolation I was incredibly happy being there. But Foulad had said that I wasn't supposed to be there. It was really odd and disconcerting. I was in paradise but I couldn't be with all the people that I wanted to be with.

I decided to go for a swim to clear my head as much as I could. I had always loved swimming and it was a wonderful feeling to be able to do so in this paradise. I dived into the pool and swam some lengths. It was extremely refreshing and I loved the feeling of the water on my skin. Finally, I decided to get out of the pool and as I did I felt as though something had changed but I wasn't quite sure what. But I knew I was ready to face whatever it was. Feeling in a relaxed state of mind, I walked back into my house to lie down in my bedroom. And that's when I started to hear the sound of a voice.

It was distant at first and seemed to fade in and out of my consciousness. I could hear something but I wasn't quite sure what. And then a short while later it came back. This time it was stronger and more persistent. It was a lovely, melancholic voice. I had never heard such clarity before. The only way to describe it was that it sounded real but otherworldly at the same time. It was as though it had been practised and it would just come and go and then come and go again. I quickly realised that I knew who the voice belonged to. It was Nilu's voice.

'I love you Daddy,' she said, over and over again.

The next thing I knew I was waking up in hospital. I had awoken from my coma. I opened my eyes. It was difficult to see at first, but as they adjusted to the light, Sheida came into focus. She was facing away from me so I tried to speak to get her attention. I opened my mouth but I just couldn't get any words out. For a few moments I felt powerless, but Sheida sensed something and she turned around. When she saw that I had woken up, her face was an absolute picture. She rushed over to embrace me and at the same time Nilu came over to me and did the same thing. It was very emotional for all of us and the embraces lasted quite a while. I was just so glad to see my wife and my daughter. I had this pang in my heart because I hadn't known whether I would ever see them again.

I felt that I wasn't quite myself and there was this strange sense of two worlds colliding. But I knew that seeing both of them meant that I was back in the real world. I knew that I was alive. What I didn't know was that in some ways my journey had only just begun.

Waking up

- *Sheida* -

The doctors had thought that the cracked ribs had lifted far enough out of the lungs so that if they removed his breathing tube Mahmoud would now be able to breathe normally and unassisted. He would find it difficult but they were worried that if the breathing tube stayed in any longer it would damage his vocal cords.

Taking the tube out was a huge moment. I waited with baited breath to see what would happen and I couldn't wait for him to come round. But nothing did happen at first. I realised that it might take some time for him to recover and after a short while I was distracted by my own thoughts and my gaze momentarily dropped. But sensing something I looked back towards him. He was awake! He was coughing and his eyes were still blurred but he was definitely awake. I embraced him and for the first time since he had been in hospital, he squeezed my hand. He could understand what we were saying and he nodded every time I talked to him. He started to move his hands. And his legs. All these were great indications that he was really back with us. After being in the coma for such a long time, at first he wasn't totally aware of his surroundings. He would open his eyes and I would talk to him but after a few minutes he would close his eyes again and fall back asleep. He found it very difficult to speak because of the breathing tube that had been in his throat. But after such a long time, the relief at seeing Mahmoud come out of the coma was almost indescribable. Just to see him breathing on his own seemed like a miracle in itself.

Everyone was amazed at his recovery and doctors continued to do more tests and checks on his injuries. Because of the prolonged intubation, they wanted him to be very careful regarding his throat and they didn't want him to try and force his voice by speaking too soon. But Mahmoud was very determined and soon after coming out of the coma, after a few attempts, he managed to get his first words out.

'Where am I?' he said, his eyes flooding with tears.

During the time that he was in the induced coma there were periods when it had seemed like there was just no hope. But for now it looked like my prayers in the evening and the day had been answered. Of course I was amazed that he had come through everything. But it didn't mean that everything was now okay. In fact the whole thing had now moved on to the next stage and I had a few questions of my own. Was he fully recovered? Now he was out of the coma, what was going to happen with his other injuries?

Over the next few days he did a lot of sleeping. Various visitors came in to see him and he drifted in and out of consciousness whilst they were there. During the coma his legs had swollen because of the lack of movement in his bed and at one point Mahmoud's brother, Masoud, and his sons, Kayvan and Amir, came over from the States to visit him. Mahmoud was moved from his bed to a special chair and his two nephews massaged his legs to reduce the swelling and get his circulation flowing. After experiencing so many low moments, it was fantastic to see such a sweet one.

A few days later the ICU private room was needed and he was transferred to the orthopaedic ward. I knew that there was still a long way to go, but at last he was getting better.

Just An Illusion

I had come back from heaven and now I was in hell. I was still in St Mary's and for the first time since I had been in the hospital I could remember being there. But it felt like a semi-reality. What was happening to me? I had returned from a place where life was simple and beautiful to a world that was even more confusing than the one I had left before the accident.

All I knew was that I kept on having these terrible illusions. I would go through days of having them and it was like living in a slow motion of the past. It was a very odd situation. I kept on thinking that I was doing something that I wasn't actually doing. One moment it seemed as though I was surrounded by one group of people but then the next moment they wouldn't be there at all. And then I would have a moment where I was trying to look for where I lived but I wasn't really in that place. It was all very strange. This was my state of mind in the hospital. I knew I wasn't in heaven anymore and I knew that I was back in the real world. But it wasn't the same world that I had known pre-accident, which was very disconcerting. A world which was once so familiar was now throwing up an unpredictability that I hadn't encountered before. Although I seemed to be okay in the daytime, it was at night-time when there was nobody else around, that the problems really began.

One night I was lying in bed when all of a sudden it was pouring with rain and there was a great flood and people appeared from nowhere and seemed to be fleeing from it. Somehow I was protected because I was in this room. In this illusionary state I was somewhere else completely and with people that I didn't know. It was as though I was now in another age with the architecture and the people around me wearing clothing that reflected the Victorian era. A lovely woman on this horse and carriage began to acknowledge me and then before I knew what was happening, I peed myself. It just went on and on and gallon after gallon of pee washed over my bed. It was horrible and scary and all I could think of was that I wanted to speak to Sheida.

I was taken to a dormitory and there was a nurse there who was assigned to look after me. She was very cold and aloof and I was very afraid and scared of what might happen next. I asked her who I was and she just told me that I knew who I was. I asked her where my mobile phone was and she said that she had it. This seemed very strange but then she gave me the phone. At first, I didn't believe it was mine because in my state of confusion I wasn't entirely sure what was real and what wasn't. But then I remembered that I had Sheida's number in my mobile and I dialled it to see what would happen. The line connected and the number started ringing.

'Why are you calling me at this time of the morning?' Sheida demanded as she answered my call. 'You frighten me when you call at this time of the day because I think that something has happened.'

It was two or three o'clock in the morning and I had clearly not only disturbed her but worried her with the timing of the call. But I was so relieved to just hear her voice because I knew that it meant I was back alive again. In the other world, although I had not understood everything at first, I had at least found clarity in my thinking. I had been certain of my surroundings and myself. But this was a total nightmare and the boundaries between reality and illusion were completely blurred. The whole experience was the exact opposite of being in the other world in that it made me feel extremely uncomfortable both in body and in mind.

When I was having a lucid moment I knew that I had lived in the real world all my life, that I had been involved in an accident, that I had been in a coma, that I had gone up to heaven and then had returned to what I knew was physically the real world. But in other moments I was totally confused and it felt like I was living in a hybrid state. I lost all track of time and what was actually only a few hours passing would feel like a week had gone by. My new world was very turbulent. It seemed like some of the time I was living in a Victorian drama but then I would shake out of it because I would be woken up by a nurse because it was time to have some food. It was very disturbing and although I tried to make some sense of it I was really worried about what was going to happen to me. I was helpless and I was all on my own. The only thing that kept me grounded was when I talked to Sheida. I was so happy to talk to her because then I knew that I was alive. I wondered whether the medication that I was being given was causing some kind of mental trauma but in effect it just made things scary because everything was all so surreal.

This strange hybrid world was incredibly eerie. Any minute I could be in a garden or grounds that were contained in the hospital. I thought that everything there was real but then I realised it wasn't because something would happen that would snap me out if it. And then the whole process would start all over again. The one thing that really helped was when all my family and friends came to visit me. When that happened I was okay as I knew where I was. Seeing Sheida, Nilu, Shabaz, Merhdad and other family and friends not only lifted my spirits it was actually vital to keeping me sane. Otherwise it was turbulent, confusing and scary and there were many times when I thought that I was actually losing my mind.

The other thing I feared was that when I was on my own I kept on thinking that Sheida was being unfaithful to me. That was a very strong emotion. In reality of course my poor wife was just taking a well-earned rest from me. I had male friends that would visit me which was fantastic and I was so pleased to see them. And then they would leave and my mind would get so twisted that if Sheida wasn't with me I would think that she must be with them. It was a period of totally insecurity on my part. At one point I actually accused her of being unfaithful. Quite rightly she put me in my place for having such thoughts and more importantly for daring to accuse her! She couldn't have been more loving and supportive and yet I had accused her of something terrible. But it was as if I just couldn't control this incredible insecurity that kept invading my personality.

I wasn't really sure what was happening with the illusions or what to do about them. I was in a state of semi-reality which was incredibly unsettling. Did everyone around me know what was happening, what I was going through, or was just I trapped in my own little world? All I knew was that having fought through my coma and having survived my various life-threatening injuries, I couldn't cope with the power that these illusions possessed. They were stronger than me. I was living what I can only describe as an illusionary life. It couldn't have been more different to the other world that I had gone to when I was in my coma, with all its beauty, peacefulness and vitality of life.

And I was thinking a lot about death. The first death that I could remember had taken place when I was five years old whilst at my grandfather's estate north of Tehran. Generations of our extended family, including uncles, aunts and cousins, would regularly gather together for great celebrations at a grand, expansive marquee in the estate's grounds. The air was always filled with chatter and laughter and the feasts would make fantastic spectacles.

And then one morning after one such occasion my brother, younger cousins and I all awoke to discover that we were on our own. The marquee was deserted and the huge garden and surrounding area was eerily silent. We didn't know where everybody was or what was going on. I got up and discovered that the only people left apart from us were the gardeners. I asked one of them what had happened and was told that my great-grandmother, the wife of the king, had died. All the adults had left and had gathered at my great-grandmother's house to be with her body. I was very scared and didn't really know what to do or who to turn to. After a few hours the adults all returned and they were now all wearing black and in mourning. It was my first experience of someone dying and I wasn't sure what to make of it all.

But despite the thoughts of death that were on my mind, the main issue that I had was the frustration of living in this semi-reality. I was certain that some things had happened. I knew that my brother had come over to see me with my two nephews. I had reached out to kiss them but I hadn't had the power to get close to them. I had been too weak to respond and have a conversation with them. And that was the last thing that I could remember about my brother and nephews being in London. It was a fleeting memory amongst all the chaos in my head caused by all the illusions that I was having.

Why were the illusions happening? I was aware that I was on strong medication to moderate my diabetes. And I was taking other antibiotics as well because of my continuing struggles with septicaemia which kept on re-occurring. The blood clot on my brain was slowly getting better but it was clearly still affecting me. All these elements were contributing to my semi-delusional state and were all possible causes of why I was having the illusions. But knowing why they were happening was one thing and stopping them was quite another.

I wasn't in a good state and was very depressed. In the other world I had felt young, vibrant surrounded by peace and tranquillity. Here I had multiple injuries, my body was in pieces and this world was anything but peaceful. And despite all the physical trauma that my body had been through it was really my mind that was cracking up. I was trying as hard as I could to hold onto something, to grasp some kind of reality but it was extremely difficult and there were some very dark days. The truth of it was that I had found my personal heaven in the other world. So why had I come back to this?

Christmas Day

- *Sheida* -

Mahmoud had made a remarkable recovery. The doctors had initially thought that he would need five operations during the first few days after the accident. With all his injuries, the complications that followed and considering his age, he had only been given the slimmest chance of survival. I had this feeling that the doctors and nurses had thought that he wouldn't even get through the first week but they had done an incredible job. Against all the odds he had somehow survived.

Now he was in the orthopaedic ward and attention turned to his hip and knee. But again, just like the ribs, the injuries seemed to be getting better on their own accord. The doctors were simply amazed. I'm not sure that they had seen this happen before. We discussed what the next steps were going to be and agreed that because Mahmoud had just come out of his coma having had a major spine operation, the other injuries would be given more time to see if the progress continued.

During this time Mahmoud was not aware of what was going on. If I asked him a few questions, the next day he wouldn't even remember if I had been there. We were all of course delighted that he could communicate in some way having come out of the coma, but not being able to register what we were saying was quite frustrating for everyone. He was completely confused and his short-term memory was just not there. He couldn't remember the accident and he couldn't even remember why he had gone to

Tesco's in the first place. He had the strength of will to get better but then he would tell me that he wasn't going to be a normal person. So I could tell by his conversation that not everything was okay in his world. After a week in the orthopaedic ward he still didn't really know where he was. I hadn't thought that he was actually ready to come out of the ICU but he had been transferred and the orthopaedic ward was his home for now.

***

It was Christmas Day 2015 and I spent the morning with my daughter and her family. Samira was very good at organising the running order of the day and although it seemed strange not having Mahmoud there, it also felt good just to have a little bit of normality in my life. For once, everything around me seemed quite calm and under control. Of course my grandchildren, Sandy, Scarlett and Savannah, were excited – it was Christmas after all – but that was how it should be. They opened their presents, my son-in-law, Jake, opened his favourite Veuve Clicquot champagne and after toasting Mahmoud's health, we all sat down to a wonderful, traditional Christmas lunch of turkey with all the trimmings. We always made a point of watching the Queen's speech after lunch and her measured delivery continued the calm sensibility of the day. After the speech had finished, Jake took me to St Mary's to see Mahmoud. He offered to come in with me, but I declined, knowing that they had other guests coming over. Besides, I was in good spirits and after such a lovely day with the family, I was hoping that Mahmoud would also be in good heart and that we would be able to have a nice, relaxed conversation. I entered the orthopaedic ward and noticed that all the beds were occupied. Nobody wanted to be in hospital, especially at Christmas but at least there were a few festive decorations up to give the place some cheer. Samira and family had also given me a piece of Christmas pudding for Mahmoud as a token of their love and support. I carried on walking up the ward, blissfully unaware of what I would find up ahead.

When I reached Mahmoud's bed, I was greeted by a scene of chaos. Mahmoud had torn open his gown and ripped the catheter tube out of his body. Urine was now accumulating in his kidney and without the tube there was no way to drain it. It was extremely serious and potentially life-threatening. I tried engaging with him but his eyes had rolled back into his head and he was getting delirious. In desperation I looked around for some help. I saw the ward Sister across the room and rushed over to her.

'You have to do something,' I protested. 'My husband is dying.'

'We're very busy, it's Christmas Day and we don't have enough staff,' she replied.

'Yes but somebody should have checked him. He's torn his gown, the tube is on the floor and his blood is mixing with his urine,' I persisted.

Hearing this news she looked concerned and together we hurried back over to his bed. It wasn't a moment too soon as it was close to becoming a catastrophe. The Sister changed his tube and was joined by a staff nurse. They tried to make the necessary adjustments to help him whilst I focused on trying to get his attention.

'Mahmoud, Mahmoud,' I shouted at him, trying to rouse him and bring him back into the present.

'Ahhhhh…' he groaned and just stared blankly at the ceiling. It was very frightening and after all we had been through I was really scared about what was happening. I could see that the Sister was worried but she and her staff managed to get the situation under control. After a few hours he settled down and returned back to some sort of stability. But he was clearly still not himself. They ran some tests and discovered that he had septicaemia. He was put on strong antibiotics and he was transferred to another room on the ward to prevent infection.

It felt like I was living on a complete rollercoaster. A high would be followed by a low and then vice versa. I was extremely worried as it just seemed that one thing was happening after another. I wasn't sure if it was ever going to end. By now I was running on empty and was completely exhausted, but somehow I managed to keep myself going.

Working Life

I had been in St Mary's for several months whilst I recuperated. During this period I was slowly trying to come to terms with what had happened to me and my visit to the other world. I hadn't told anybody about it and I was still trying to figure out what the point of it all had been. I knew that I wasn't myself yet although at least the illusions were now becoming less frenetic. But the time I was spending in hospital had given me the opportunity to reflect on a lot of things and I began to think about what I had achieved in my working life.

In 1964 I was in Tehran and working for the Iranian government at the Plan Organisation researching land management and agricultural improvement. Ironically to some extent it was what I would have been doing anyway for my grandfather's estate before the Shah's intervention. But I knew this particular work was futile without any funding and I was frustrated and needed a change. I would go to work in the morning and come back in the evening and not feel that I ever really achieved anything.

The whole thing had just become one big yawn. It didn't seem to matter what reports I wrote or who I spoke to, the truth was that without investment everything was just going to stay the same. It was around this time that I heard news that there were two British gentlemen who were looking for a British-educated engineer. They were staying in the Park Hotel which was owned by the father of my friend Farhad Diba and at the time was the biggest hotel in Iran. I asked Farhad to arrange a meeting and duly went over to the hotel to see them.

Ambrose Congreve owned an engineering company called Humphreys and Glasgow (H&G) and Sir Charles Strafford was his travelling companion. Mr Congreve was looking to overseas to expand operations. He had been at Trinity and when we met he couldn't believe he had found another Trinity graduate, especially in Iran. It was a good start and he thought that I would be good material for his future Middle Eastern planning. The meeting progressed and we discussed my potential role. I told them that I already had a good job that I couldn't be sacked from – which remarkably was true – and that if it was just some kind of experiment on their part then I wasn't interested. I couldn't promise what I could do for them, but they could be assured that I would give them my absolute best in anything that I did. They seemed to like my candour and I was invited to London for an interview.

I was interviewed by Derek Lennon, one of the nicest and fairest men you could ever meet, in H&G's sumptuous offices in Carlisle Place, Victoria Street. Ambrose Congreve was a collector of antiques and the offices were furnished with antique chairs and paintings. The interview went well and I was offered the job. Extremely happy, I accepted the offer, which left me with two issues that I had to deal with.

The first issue was that I hadn't yet resigned from the Plan Organisation. I had lots of friends there and I found it very embarrassing to have to resign. But I knew it was the right time for me to leave and get out and try something new and on my return to Tehran I went to see my boss to tell him the news. When I told him about the job that I was going to, his reaction surprised me. He said that he didn't blame me for leaving and in fact was quite envious. He had lots of ongoing problems with the Shah and they didn't seem as though they were going to go away anytime soon. And when I told my parents they were delighted for me. I had been working for the most prestigious organisation in Iran, but they thought that I could do more with my life.

The second issue was that I didn't know anything about petrochemicals or construction engineering. This was a bit of a harder challenge to overcome, but my new boss, Derek Lennon, gave me a six month crash course and I quickly got up to speed. I had been one of the first Iranians to leave Iran and improve my prospects by getting a job overseas, but when my friends saw my success, they followed suit and a lot of them ended up kickstarting their careers by getting jobs in America.

My job title at H&G was a simple one: to run the Middle East! But the challenge was a huge one. At that time nobody in Iran had heard of H&G and I really had to sell who we were to the oil and gas companies. But I was determined to put us on the map and compete with the big boys in the industry who were more established, such as Foster Wheeler, Kellogg Brown & Root, and Bechtel. My first task was to endear myself with potential clients and get H&G listed amongst the bidders. Four companies were normally invited to bid for a project and I made phone call after phone in my bid to get us noticed and become one of the four. It wasn't easy and I became a bit of a nuisance as I wouldn't take no for an answer. Although it was slow progress at first, I was relentless in my approach and at the age of twenty-eight I was made a director of the company. I travelled around the world meeting and negotiating with major corporations.

I went to New York and stayed for three months at the Plaza Hotel whilst we bid on a huge contract with Amoco for the construction of an oil terminal at Kharg Island, just off the coast of Iran. It was an exciting time and I loved the pitching and negotiating the work entailed. Their New York headquarters had an intriguing address and each day I would make the walk over from the hotel to their offices for meetings at 666 Fifth Avenue. I socialised with their executives, playing tennis and going out to multiple dinners with them. I did everything that I possibly could to get the contract but ultimately we couldn't compete with the Japanese on price and the contract went to Mitsui. But I felt inspired in my work and within my first three years at H&G we landed three huge contracts to build petrochemical installations in Iran. One of them in particular, was an interesting experience.

I was always looking to create contacts with the aim of getting the next big deal. I would work hard on my networking, knowing that some contacts would pay off and some wouldn't. But at least if I tried my best to make something happen I was in the game so to speak. One of the contacts I worked on most was Mostofi, the Chairman of the NPC, the National Petrochemical Company of Iran. The Shah had decreed that he wanted to develop Iran's petrochemical industry and so everybody wanted to do business with NPC and they were the bread and butter of all petrochemical contracting companies. It was a hugely competitive time with everyone looking for an edge to get a deal done. My family and Mostofi's were both close and his nephews were at university with my brother, so I knew him very well and I tried my hardest to do some business with him but all to no avail. I was determined, but he would always tell me that I had to lower my prices or be more competitive. I began to get a bit frustrated and there didn't seem to be anything more I could do. And then one morning I received a phone call.

'Mahmoud, we are going to build a fertiliser plant in Shiraz and I want to see if we can negotiate it with Humphreys and Glasgow,' a familiar voice said.

'Would you like to repeat that again please?' I replied, trying to keep the excitement out of my voice. I had hoped that we might be invited to bid for the job but this was a different story. I couldn't really believe it but it was true. The call ended and I phoned Derek Lennon in London immediately.

'How would you like to negotiate with NPC over building a new fertiliser plant,' I said to him.

'That would be great, but they don't negotiate,' he replied.

'Yes they do.'

My hard work and networking skills had finally paid off and I celebrated with a few drinks at The Pub. The next day I flew over to London to negotiate a $50 million deal with NPC. In 1977 this was a huge contract and was the first time NPC had negotiated with one company directly as opposed to offering up the contract for tender. Getting it over the line was an amazing coup for me and for Humphreys and Glasgow and the new Urea plant meant that the Iranian economy would benefit as fertilisers wouldn't have to be imported from abroad anymore.

Ambrose Congreve had given me a start but he was an imposing figure and I was quite afraid of him. You always felt that he might meet you in the corridor and sack you if he didn't like the colour of your tie. It seemed to have the desired effect on me at any rate as my career went from strength to strength. But not everybody was so keen on Mr Congreve's 'blue-eyed boy'. H&G had 1,100 people working for them and amongst them was a Mr Davies who was effectively the MD. He was extremely jealous of my success in the company and my social standing living in Knightsbridge, but even he had to acknowledge that whatever I was doing was working. The jealousy didn't last because he was fired not long after I joined. I was with H&G from 1964 to 1974. During this period Iran had nationalised the oil industry and the Shah had negotiated a very good deal with the OPEC countries who were in Iran. Oil prices began to shoot up and with huge investment, Iran became littered with petrodollars. I was looking after Iraq, Libya, Saudi Arabia and Kuwait. These countries had stable leaders at the time and so it was still possible to do business there. I managed to get us a great contract for a fertiliser plant at Homs in Syria.

It was a time of great excess in the industry with multimillion dollar deals taking place and the personal peccadillos of the rich and powerful being indulged. On one occasion I was invited to a meeting at one of London's top hotels with the head of one of the Middle East's premier petrochemical companies. He was a controversial character who owed the London casinos a great deal of money and our meeting took place in a huge private suite. We discussed the possibility of a potential deal and then during the conversation a slightly odd thing happened. The suite doors opened and we were joined by a steady procession of handsome young men. They didn't join us but I was definitely conscious of their presence. Aware of my host's reputation within the industry, I talked through the deal for a while longer before making my excuses and leaving him and his friends to conduct their own business.

In 1974 Ambrose Congreve had to leave H&G because of tax reasons. It was time for me to leave as well and I went back to Iran. I had built up some amazing contacts and was happy to be a freelance consultant. But the country had changed so much. It was now a hotbed of commerce and the hotels were so full that in my father's hotel, several businessmen who had come to Tehran for meetings ended up sleeping in the sauna.

They were happy memories of a time spent working hard and playing hard. I had always been an active person who had gone out and done things. It was another frustrating aspect of being stuck in hospital for so long. But good though the memories were, they were just that and my working life and exploits were now part of my past life. I looked around at my immediate surroundings from my hospital bed and I began to wonder what life had in store for me from now on. There had to be more to my life than just this. At seventy-eight years old I wasn't exactly looking for another job, but I was searching for a purpose.

Resilience

– Nilu –

One of the hardest things to juggle throughout the whole drama was trying to spend enough time with everyone who needed it. I had added complications in that at various points I actually had both my parents in the hospital at the same time. As well as Dad being in St Mary's, Paddington, my mother was suffering from cancer and was also in hospital, but in Parkside, Wimbledon. Living in South East London I was, along with my family, caught somewhere in the middle.

Along with taking care of two small boys it was incredibly difficult to manage the situation. I was always having to listen to two set of different doctors and process everything that they were saying. Throw in having to do a job at the same time and it was a pretty horrendous period that affected everyone, although my husband gave me great support as did my sister, who shared the load with my mother's illness.

To try and help keep up spirits on visits to see Dad, I would sometimes bring my small boys with me, but I was often on my own and of course it wouldn't be long before they were running round the hospital. So in the end we had to stop their visits. I would talk to Dad as much as I could and I would say things like 'Hi Dad. It's me. I love you. You're amazing. We'll get through this.' I don't know whether he heard me or not but it felt comforting to do so.

When we realised the extent of his injuries it really hit me hard and I was worried about what was going to happen to him. I always thought of him as being so strong, whether he was walking, playing tennis or swimming in the sea. Would he ever be the same again? When they took the tube out and he eventually started speaking, even though his voice was much softer, it was incredible to hear it. I tried to be stoical in both my thoughts and actions, but there were times when I thought that it was truly terrible what had happened and felt really sorry for him. But I didn't want to give the sense that anyone around him was *breaking* as it were. I felt like he needed strength rather than pity.

Although it may sound strange, it felt like the accident brought his family together. Dad had struggled with his personal relationship with his sister and on occasions with his brother and in a way it's curious that the three siblings have had so many wars between them. They both visited him and it felt like the accident healed a lot of those wounds. His sister sat with him in the hospital and they talked and realised they had clearly both made enormous mistakes that neither of them had admitted to. It was like a grace period where Dad forgave people. I wanted to maintain relationships with my cousins, my nephews and my aunt so I had to be incredibly neutral about any of the disagreements between them all, which was not always that easy to do.

What Dad has always had is this real strength. He's very resilient and whatever happens to him he just has this amazing ability to bounce back, dust himself off and go again. Without that drive I'm not sure he would have been able to get through the accident and everything surrounding it. I'm not sure that anyone would have been able to do so.

Resilience appears to be a family trait. My eldest son, who is now seven, was born at twenty-six weeks, spent three months in an incubator and 125 days in hospital. He also survived an earthquake. He's an absolute fighter. Just like my father.

Family Ties

I was still in hospital and trying to re-engage with the real world. My mind was pretty scrambled and it was difficult to get a complete picture of where exactly I was at. I would have moments when everything would come together and then times when everything seemed to be all over the place. But it was during this period that I came across a wonderful poem based on a piece of prose by David Harkins. It was so strong and meaningful and made a tremendous mark on me. On one level I couldn't really understand why I was still alive and the poem made me think about what I had been through in my own life. I was still in a very confused state and I thought that if I had died that I would have been forgotten about.

After reading the poem a few times I was so moved by it that I changed the emphasis in it to reflect my own situation. The new version was meant for Sheida and Nilu. I had been thinking about them as I read the poem and I hoped that this would help them to understand what I was thinking. It was a beautiful poem and seemed to say everything that I wanted to say but my mind would not allow.

I was concerned about the world that I had come back to, but was still very reflective and having considered my working life I now started to think about my parents again. Seeing all the houses in the other world had made me think about the life that they had enjoyed in Tehran. It was a wonderful life that had been rudely interrupted.

In 1980 the Shah had been overthrown and the country had been overtaken by the clergy. It had ramifications for my whole family but the first to feel the effects was my brother. He was a successful urologist and ran his own hospital in Tehran. But he was worried about the new regime and wanted a good education for his children and so decided to leave for London with his family. In retrospect this was a bad decision as doctors and surgeons were hugely respected, even by the clergy and as a result those stayed who were not adversely affected by the new regime.

The Iranian revolution hadn't directly affected me like the rest of my family as I was already in London, but it had meant that I had lost my power base in Iran. This was a problem as Iran was my biggest market in the oil industry. I had built up a huge network of contacts and knew everybody there from the prime minister to the local traders. But for my parents things became far more extreme under the new regime. Tehran was now in chaos and every day regime officials were trying to confiscate whatever you owned. I tried to persuade my parents to leave the country because if you were found to have any connections to the deposed royal family you were likely to be imprisoned or executed. At the time, nobody quite knew if those 'rulings' extended to those with links to the Qajar dynasty and my parents continued to be fearful as to what would happen to them the longer they stayed. I was worried about them but they just did not want to leave. But once the new regime had forcibly taken over my father's hotels there was no turning no back and they hurriedly left Tehran and joined me in London.

I was living in our large house in Rutland Gate, Knightsbridge and if I'm honest I wasn't quite prepared for what followed. First of all my mother and father arrived. Then my brother and his wife and their three children. And finally my sister and her husband plus their two children. We were very lucky in that the house could accommodate such a large number of people, but having them there had a major impact on both me and the London bachelor lifestyle that I had created for myself. It felt like a family invasion!

After a year my brother couldn't take it in London anymore. He was working as a surgeon but he had gone from running his own hospital in Tehran with all the prestige and responsibility that brought, to working in London and just making up the numbers and hardly being paid anything. And so he got a very good job in a New York hospital and he and his family left to live in Long Island. Then my sister and family were given permission to emigrate to Australia and my brother-in-law got a job in banking in Sydney and my sister started working for the media magnate, Kerry Packer.

One of the enigmas of the revolution was that Iranians were free to leave the country and did not appear to have any restrictions travelling. It was very strange and nobody could understand it. In other countries that had gone through political turmoil such as Iraq, Afghanistan and Syria, the first thing that the new regime had done was to stop freedom of movement and travelling. But it never happened in Iran. In all the upheaval my family endured with the regime change, it was one of the few things that made life easier.

I knew exactly what made my parents happy and gave them a life which went some way towards negating the horrendous impact that the Iranian revolution had had on their lives. My father had been a wealthy man who had owned hotels and apartment blocks but they were all taken away from him when the clergy had risen to power. Luckily he had possessed the acumen to deposit a few hundred thousand pounds in England and so after they came over to London, they were able to live out their days in comfort.

He used to loving gambling and I would take him to the Clermont club every Saturday night. The waiters there adored him and on his seventieth birthday they produced a bottle of wine which was seventy years old. It was like treacle! But the fact that they went and got it for him was an incredibly kind gesture. I used to bring my father to Queen's three times a week to watch the tennis. And I used to take him to the races to watch my horse run. He loved and embraced the lifestyle that I had created for myself in London.

I tried to give them whatever they wanted whether it was a grand gesture or something small. They used to love some of the

TV programmes of the time such as *Dallas*, *Dynasty* and *The Golden Girls*, but they couldn't speak English very well so I used to interpret them for them and it would be the pinnacle of their day. All I wanted to do was to make them happy and ease some of the pain of what had happened to them. On the whole they had different interests but sometimes their tastes did overlap. My mother used to love going to Harrods and my father sometimes went to the Harrods Food Hall three times a day. Much to my mother's exasperation he would buy fresh meat or delicacies on each visit, even when there was no more room to store them at home. I always thought that there was another reason that he went there so often and I'm sure that the fact that Harrods was always full of beautiful girls, whether serving or shopping, didn't escape his notice. He had been a very good-looking man in his youth and had always enjoyed the company of beautiful women.

My father was the most responsible and caring person that you could ever meet. Whenever we really needed something he would always support us. But although he was a highly sensitive, loving man, he found it very difficult to show his emotions. He came from Rasht in the north of Iran. His father was a wealthy merchant who used to trade with the Russians in Baku and my father spoke fluent Russian as well as Persian.

Each year my parents would visit either my brother in New York or my sister in Sydney. They would spend at least a few weeks with them, but the rest of the time they would prefer to stay in London. In 1986, my father, eighty years old, went on a solo trip to visit my sister and her family in Sydney. One night, as they were going out to dinner he developed a headache and then without warning suffered a massive brain haemorrhage. He was taken to hospital but sadly he died three days later.

Years later my sister took my mother and me to visit his grave at the Muslim cemetery where he was buried. A few years before, my brother-in-law's father, Mr Monajami, had also visited the family in Sydney and had dropped dead in the middle of the street. Uncannily he and my father were buried side by side in the same cemetery. We arrived at the cemetery and as we neared his grave my mother became highly emotional. I held my mother's hand and tried to give her strength but deep down I was devastated myself. My father had always kept an emotional distance between the two of us. Over the course of our lives I would have loved to have hugged and kissed him a thousand times but sadly it never happened. I was left extremely frustrated that I was never able to break through the veneer.

My mother lived a very full life. She loved roses and I would take her to the Rose Garden in Regent's Park. She would meet for teas with various cousins from the Qajar dynasty that lived in London and they would share a cultural similarity and talk about the life that they knew. She was to have her own life-changing operation when she had open-heart surgery. My poor brother kept on saying that she didn't need to have the operation because she was pretty active and could survive through medication. Being a surgeon he knew the risks and was scared of the possibility of having a stroke. But my sister thought that our mother should do what she wanted to do. My mother went ahead with the operation but sadly had a stroke soon afterwards. It took her five years to get over the stroke but eventually she managed it. She was a highly determined Qajar princess and used that drive to get herself back to normality.

My mother loved doing chores around the house. On Saturdays we both would go to Portobello market to see if there was anything that caught her eye for the house. I couldn't believe how well she was doing after her stroke. Everything seemed to be back to normal both linguistically and physically. Then on one Monday I was in the office and Nilu called me to say she had fallen and now had cramp and couldn't move. I rushed over to them and she was lying there in pain and it was obvious she was not okay. I called an ambulance and when they arrived they said that she had broken her hip. I knew that was a disaster. She was taken to what was then just Westminster hospital and they operated on her. I called my brother and he flew over the next day. And then she started to go through recuperation and physiotherapy, but she died five days later.

She was such a big part of my life. She lived next door to me and I looked after her and saw her every day. We had brought over an Iranian maid from Tehran to help her, but our mother and son bond was such that I couldn't even go on holiday because she was so insecure that she wouldn't let me go. Her death devastated me and it took me two years to get over it.

***

My brother and sister had visited me in hospital and I had quite different relationships with both of them. Masoud and I were very close growing up. He was two years older than me and the age difference was just enough to stop it being competitive. When I had gone back to Iran whilst working for Humphrey's and Glasgow I had made some money on a few deals that I had worked on. My brother's surgical career had yet to take off and I found myself in a position where I could help him out financially. So that's what I did. He was very grateful because at that point in his life he was only just starting out. Eventually he would have a long and distinguished career which would include becoming the Shah's personal urologist. I had always been close with my brother. But like all siblings we had had our ups and downs as well.

My sister and I have always had a fractious relationship. I used to shower her with gifts when she was younger but our relationship changed when she took over our last property in Iran. For seven years of my life my sister remained in Iran whilst I was growing up in England. She came over at fifteen years of age and went to a school in Carmarthen, Wales, to learn English for a year. I then received a letter from my parents asking me to find a school for her. At that point I was in my first job after Cambridge as a trainee working for Fisons in East Anglia. I discovered that there was this incredible school on a cliff top by the sea called Felixstowe College. I wrote to the school and managed to arrange to see the headmistress.

Having recounted my experiences at Cambridge I managed to make a good impression on my sister's behalf and she was granted an interview. When the big day came I accompanied her to the school. My sister was very intelligent and could speak fluent English by now, but she was very *green* and found the atmosphere a bit overwhelming. It was also a very prestigious school and in those days there weren't that many foreigners of any description, let alone Iranians, to be found in Suffolk. So we were slightly up against it, but I was able to smooth our way through the interview and help my sister by encouraging her to respond to questions and make a good account of herself. It seemed to do the trick and she was offered a place then and there.

When my parents died I was responsible for dividing everything into three for my sister, my brother and myself. I was in charge of everything, the distribution of the will.

I sold my flat in London and wanted to invest the money. I put large amount of the proceeds into a bond in Iran which had a 25% interest rate. This provided a fantastic return and an income of over one hundred thousand pounds a year. But there was trouble looming.

In 2007 when President Bush put sanctions on Iran, it created huge problems for the Iranian economy. Food was smuggled into Iran or it was overpaid for and came into the country through Dubai. Eventually the country's economy was so stretched that they started to devalue the rial. The reason for doing that was because of the income the government received from the oil. If they devalued the rial they got more money for the foreign exchange and government employees were paid through that.

This gave me a real dilemma. The interest rate remained the same and you were getting more money from your bond than you would do if you took it out. So I kept it in. Over about a month the currency devalued by 70% and I was left with a fraction of my initial investment. I was devastated. It was a major haemorrhage and had a huge impact on my life.

Although I found it difficult to remember things on a day to day basis, the memories of my working life, family and childhood had somehow remained in my head and I found it a strangely cathartic process to go through everything and think about all the things that had happened in my life. My recovery was taking an age and I was nowhere near where I wanted to be but I did feel like that at last, I was beginning to get back on my feet.

Comeback Of The Century
– *Prince Shabaz* –

When I saw Mahmoud in St Mary's after he had come out of the coma it was a great relief. Of course we were all concerned beforehand because of the blood clot he had on his brain. We didn't know whether he would come round at all, but when he did we weren't quite sure whether he would be compos mentis or not. So the fact that he was speaking at all was a great sign.

But it was very difficult to understand him. Time didn't seem to mean anything to him and there was no structure to what he was talking about. One moment he would seem quite lucid and the next he would be off talking about something which made little sense. It made it very difficult to have a conversation with him during those moments.

I knew immediately that it was the effect of the drugs. He was totally disorientated and his speech was all jumbled up. Of course he also had damage to his vocal chords which made his voice much softer and that didn't help either. But he had successfully come through the initial injuries and being in the coma. It was quite remarkable and I could not imagine that anyone else would have survived.

I did give some thought as to what to say when he came round. When he woke up I wasn't sure whether to be sympathetic and go down the old 'Oh Mahmoud…' route or just be natural and tease him like I normally would. I decided to go with the latter and just joke about things. He took it very well and it made him laugh. It was a very gradual process which went on for a long time. First in hospital and then eventually in rehab. The thing was to get him to walk again.

But I knew that the next stage, the rehabilitation, was going to be extremely difficult for him. At his age it was going to be very hard. You need a lot of courage to come back. You're in your late seventies and then you've got this huge battle, this mountain to climb. I didn't doubt that he had the resolve to do it, but his body had taken a massive beating and his mind was still clearly scrambled, medication or not. That was my big worry, whether he would have the courage to want to go through this incredibly difficult process. Because we weren't talking about one thing like say Douglas Bader when he lost his legs, Mahmoud had several things wrong with him. So I was really worried but was determined to be there for him and help give him the courage to do it.

It took a long time before we were able to resume a natural conversation because every time we tried there would be times when he wasn't quite sure where he was or what was going on. This went on for quite a while. The changes were imperceptible at first but eventually we made a breakthrough.

It was just like his voice. At first we thought that the tube had damaged his vocal chords post coma. He could only really whisper and you couldn't hear what he was saying. It must have been torture. He was such a great raconteur and natural storyteller and had a gift of mimicking accents. Not to be able, in effect, to be yourself would be unbelievably frustrating. So I was determined to help him in his efforts to regain it.

I watched over him and said to him that he had to do this and then do that and every time he did it and completed the exercises or made an improvement, however slight, I would applaud him. I wanted to encourage him further so he felt like people were on his case so to speak and that we weren't going to allow him to get away with anything. It was typical schoolboy stuff – come on man you can do it, that kind of thing, but because of our longstanding friendship I was able to do it. We have always been able to say anything that we want to each other. I knew how important it was because for him to lose his voice was a fate worse than death.

The main thing was his joie de vivre. He wanted really to get back on his feet. I kept telling him what any good friend would say that he had to make a comeback. But even someone as resilient as Mahmoud did occasionally have his doubts and he would sometimes voice his concerns to me and say things like that it wasn't worth it and that he would be better off dead. Instinctively, I wouldn't hear about it. I told him that he was talking nonsense and that he was going to make the comeback of the century. The biggest frustration was that it was not that dissimilar to when he was in the coma in that there really wasn't much you could do. It was very frustrating. You actually couldn't do that much apart from just show up.

The truth is that from what I saw at the beginning I thought that basically he was a goner. Deep down I never thought that he would make it back. I was determined that we weren't going to lose him, but I thought that if they had said that sadly Mahmoud had passed away I would not have been at all surprised. To me, with all the problems that he had I didn't think he could make it. The fact that he did, showed all his fighting characteristics and his joie de vivre.

The great thing was that despite everything, getting the injuries, going through the coma, losing the voice, despite all those things, he was still the same friend. He was still the same Mahmoud.

Rehab

After four months of post coma recuperation, I was signed out of St Mary's and sent to Farm Lane for rehab. Although I had been through an unbelievable ordeal, the doctors realised that rest was not enough and I now needed physiotherapy. Farm Lane in Fulham was a modern care home where this could be provided. I could hardly walk and I realised I had a great challenge ahead of me.

When I arrived they asked me what my goal was and I told them that I was going to walk out of there. I was determined to do anything that was within my power to make it happen. I couldn't really move at all on my own to start with and I had to use a walker. Each day I would walk up and down the corridors. But I would fall a lot which would cause a lot of pain and stress. Slowly I began to regain my strength. And after about a month into my rehab I was gradually making some progress. During that time more friends of mine would come and visit. I really was stunned by their generosity in giving up their time to come and see me.

One of them was an old friend from Cambridge, Simon Courtauld. We had met when he was a freshman and I was in my third year. He approached me at a restaurant in Cambridge called the Varsity which was a renowned meeting place for undergraduates and owned by a Greek guy who used to host after-hours poker evenings. Simon had heard that I was Persian and sought me out. He told me that he would love to visit my country one day and I responded that I was sure I could sort something out.

A few years after both our graduations, I was working for Ambrose Congreve and heading for Tehran whilst he had started

107

working as a journalist for the *Spectator* magazine. I contacted him and invited him to stay. I wanted to lay on the best hospitality for him and introduced him to the then prime minister as well as two ex-prime ministers at a couple of parties we attended as I thought he would appreciate meeting them. He did and had a great time. But I had underestimated him. He wanted to discover everything and everyone Iran had to offer and we set off exploring countless new and interesting places outside Tehran that I had barely heard of, let alone been to. We travelled right across the country and visited fascinating historical cities such as Isfahan and Shiraz. So whilst I provided him with great hospitality, it was because of him that I got an education about my own country.

He returned the favour a few years later. We were sharing a flat together in London and taking the social scene by storm. A friend of his had just opened a nightclub and Simon asked me whether I would like to become a founder member. Intrigued, I agreed to sign up. The friend turned out to be Mark Birley and the nightclub turned out to be Annabel's, which would become one of the most esteemed members club in London, if not the world. It became my entry into the highest echelons of London's social scene at the time. And the benefit of my early patronage was such that until very recently I was still only paying fifty pounds for the yearly membership. Being a member of such a prestigious club certainly helped my standing amongst friends. They used to call me up and ask me to reserve a table for them and as a member, I was more than happy to help them out.

Other generous friends would show their support in different ways. Rudy Alam was like a surrogate sister to me. I had known her since 1963. Her father was one of the most powerful men in Iran after the Shah and at the time was the longest-serving prime minister of Iran. She would call me every day but she couldn't come to the hospital because the hospital scenario upset her. However she would send Persian food to me during my post-coma rehab stays in hospital which gave me great comfort when it was most needed. I had supported her in other ways, many years before.

It was 1966 and we were visiting Les Ambassadeurs casino in Mayfair which at one time was a residential home of the Rothschilds. In those days it was run by John and Tiny Mills and of course in the best tradition of English nicknames, Tiny was actually six foot six. We were playing roulette in the gambling section upstairs, known as Les A. Rudy placed her bet, the wheel spun and her number came up. She had won heavily and I was congratulating her when all of a sudden we were rudely interrupted by a young Englishman in his early thirties and obviously from high society.

'That was my money on that number,' he shouted out in an exaggerated fashion. We all turned towards him.

'Actually sir, it was Miss Alam's bet,' stated the croupier who had placed it for her. The croupiers all knew Rudy and were extremely fond of her. But the outspoken Englishman continued his accusation.

'No that wog didn't place that bet. I did. Anyway she's a foreigner.'

'What did you say?' I cut across him.

'That foreigner is trying to steal my money.'

'What did you say?' I yelled into his face, barely able to control myself. I couldn't believe what he was calling my friend and was ready to do whatever it would take to put an end to it. I wasn't really one for violence but I wasn't going to stand by and let this obnoxious fool continue his horrendous insults. But before I could take things any further, the casino staff grabbed him and despite his protestations, escorted him off the premises. We learnt later that he was barred, and his membership had been cancelled. We were well-known clients of the casino and friends of the owners but that wasn't the point. I wasn't the recipient of his abuse, but as far as I was concerned, if my friend was the target, that was just as bad, if not worse. Rudy has never forgotten it and to this day she brings up the story of the time that I defended her honour.

It was not the only time that I found myself in a casino. In fact I frequented them quite a lot. I loved the competition and gambling but also the social interaction and the atmosphere. One Christmas in 1975, my parents were over visiting from Iran when the doorbell rang. I answered the door to be greeted by a 'special delivery' for a Mr Mahmoud Izadi. It appeared to be quite generous whatever it was and I instructed the delivery men to bring the large crates into the house. With great anticipation I opened them to see what was inside. Each crate contained one great surprise after another: twelve bottles of Dom Pérignon, six bottles of Chateau Rothschild, six bottles of Brane Cantenac, six bottles of Chablis, a Cartier watch and a Cartier lighter.

'What is all this?' my father inquired.

'It's a Christmas present from the Clermont Club,' I replied.

'How much bloody money did you lose this year?' he exclaimed.

The Clermont Club was the first London casino run by the renowned John Aspinall and had indeed done very well out of me that year. I happened to be friends with the PR manager Lady Joanna Bradford, a great friend of mine from my time in Norwich. I didn't tell my father how much money I had lost at the club, but I did put in a phone call to Lady Joanna to *thank* her for the gift.

'What the hell's this?' I teased, knowing full well what it was.

'Darling, you deserve it,' she purred, not missing a beat.

Iranians have a *point faible* for gambling. If you go to any house in Iran they have a night of the week where they will play cards. I loved everything about the Clermont Club with its fantastic food, service and wonderful atmosphere. My parents loved every minute of it too. When my parents came over to live in London and right up to the time of the deaths, I gave them the best times of their lives.

I still hadn't resolved what had happened regarding what I had been told about them in the other world. And it was eating away at me. I also had my own conflicts that I needed to resolve. Even if I was slowly getting better, I knew that unless I found the solution to my troubles I would never fully recover. I had to find a way to heal myself. I had to find out what this all meant.

Mahmoud Izadi

One More Time

- *Sheida* -

Mahmoud's rehab had been progressing but he wasn't out of trouble yet. On one particular day we were speaking on the phone and he told me that for the first time they had allowed him to go to the dining room and have breakfast with the others. I was happy for him as any positive stimulation was always welcome. I told him that I would see him later that day at Farm Lane as usual.

I was meeting a friend for a coffee and having got off the bus, was walking down the street when I suddenly realised that I didn't have my mobile phone. I realised that it must have slid out of its cover when I had been on the bus and that I must have left it there. I was now further down the street and the bus had pulled away from the stop but I jumped into a taxi and instructed the driver to 'follow that bus' like they do in the movies. We tailed it and followed it for a while but eventually lost it in the traffic. I knew that the bus's end destination was Willesden bus depot and so I instructed the taxi driver to head for there. We arrived and I just managed to catch the bus driver before he went off his shift. Together we searched the area on the bus where I had been sitting. But the phone was no longer there and it became obvious that somebody must have stolen it. So despite my little adventure chasing the bus across town it was all to no avail and I was left without a mobile phone.

I decided to cut my losses and headed straight for Farm Lane to see Mahmoud. But as I arrived there I could see there was

111

an ambulance outside. This was unusual and my heart began to beat a little faster. I just had a feeling that the ambulance was there for Mahmoud. As I approached it, I saw that he was being taken on a stretcher out of the rehab centre. I noticed that for some reason he was wearing red-framed glasses on top of his head. As he was being transferred into the ambulance I hurried into the centre and found one of his nurses and asked her what was happening. Only that morning he had seemed fine, talking to me about going to breakfast with the others. In the time it had taken for me to mislay my phone, everything seemed to have changed. She replied that he was delirious and that the reason they had called for an ambulance for him was because he had septicaemia. I couldn't believe it. He had septicaemia for the second time? How could this happen again? The doctor had checked Mahmoud's condition that morning and realised that he had a fever, was not with it and was completely confused. He was now completely unconscious. They rushed him to the Chelsea and Westminster Hospital and put him on all sorts of antibiotics.

It seemed like every time we made some progress we would have another setback. So far we had got through them all. But what if this was the one where that didn't happen? I didn't know what was going to happen from one minute to the next and it was incredibly draining living like this. Thankfully his septicaemia was brought under control once again and they took him back to rehab. He remained there for another four weeks.

Although the staff at Farm Lane had done a great job they were also understaffed and doctors only came to visit the rehab patients once a week. This meant that if a patient got sick like Mahmoud had done, it might not get picked up until the condition became serious and potentially life-threatening. It also meant that he was still not yet out of danger. By now I was getting used to the fact that anything might happen at any moment, but it still didn't make it less scary when something did.

Playing The Game

Tennis had been such a huge part of my life but it was another passion, gambling, which led me to my greatest sporting moment. I used to frequent Coral casinos and as a result on one occasion in 1977, I was invited to play at the Coral sponsored Pro-Am at Queen's. This was a great honour and I was partnered by professional player Bob Carmichael. For me tennis at Queen's had it all and I had been a member there since the sixties. It was a glamorous sport and was great for social interactions. I had made some fantastic friends there and I just enjoyed the game enormously. But on court I was always fighting to win and I loved the challenge of playing and trying to overcome other players.

It was a beautiful summer's day in West London. The members and their families were out in full force, the pristine grass courts were picture perfect and a slew of top players had ensured the stands were packed to capacity. I was nervous playing with such a champion player as Bob Carmichael, but he helped me raise my game to a new level. We started the tournament well, dispatching John Lloyd and Buster Mottram and their partners amongst others. From then on the matches were a mixture of easy wins and hard-fought victories until eventually we reached the final.

We were to play professional player Fred Stolle and Formula One world racing champion James Hunt. Of course Carmichael and Stolle were both fantastic players. But having seen James Hunt play I didn't think that he was any better than me and I thought I could hold my own against him.

The atmosphere was fantastic and 5,000 spectators were watching us as we got ready for the final. I got an even bigger thrill from the fact that Nilu, who was six years old at the time, was also watching me play. She couldn't believe her dad was playing on centre court. If I had thought about it too much I might not have believed it myself. The final started and it was ultra-competitive. It was neck and neck the whole way with momentum swinging back forth between each side until one particular service game when Bob Carmichael hit a couple of double faults whilst serving to James Hunt. It was a real shame because amateur players, myself included, have real problems when facing the type of kick or swinging serve a professional player can produce and double faults count for quite a lot when playing in a shortened match. But breaking Bob Carmichael's serve gave them the edge that they needed and our opponents ran out eventual winners.

It had been a privilege just to play and I still had one claim to fame afterwards. During the match I had managed to hit two winners, one forehand and one backhand, past the great Stolle. I was pretty pleased with that but more was to come as I received my greatest ever sporting compliment.

'Those are the best two shots that I've ever seen an amateur hit in my life,' Bob Carmichael remarked. I was really proud and although we had lost felt pretty good about everything. Little did I know that I was actually in for a pleasant surprise. After the tournament had finished we retired to one of Coral's casinos where amidst the celebrations I was approached by the casino manager.

'I have something for you,' he said.

'What do you mean?' I replied. I had no idea what he was talking about.

'Your winnings?' he smiled as he produced a cheque with my name on it for the sum of £3,800. With the thrill of the day and reaching the final I had completely forgotten that I had placed an each way bet on myself for £100!

'That's fantastic. Can I get it in cash?' I asked him.

The casino manager looked surprised but assured me it was not a problem. I tracked down Bob Carmichael to relay the good news.

'I've just won £3,800,' I told him. 'And even better, half of it's yours!'

He was astounded by the gesture. Professional tennis players didn't earn much money in those days and so it meant a lot to him. It rounded off an incredibly special day.

It was a great memory but back in rehab the reality was dawning on me that memories might be all that I had. I wondered whether I had a realistic chance of playing tennis again. My injuries had been so severe that it was a miracle that I had survived at all. It had been a nightmare for my family, friends and the doctors and nurses as they tried to balance my problems whilst keeping me stable enough to live. Of course I had been in my personal heaven during this time and so was unaware of all the drama. I still couldn't walk on my own yet but as usual I was reaching for the stars. I decided to have a look at my medical notes from St Mary's. In terms of my sporting prospects it didn't make for great reading:

1. Type 2 respiratory failure and respiratory failure secondary to rib fracture pain causing hyperventilation. Mr Izadi was transferred to ITU and was incubated on 4th – 17th December. Successful extubation with CPAP.
2. Acute kidney injury (Cr 400) Did not require any hemofiltration and has resolved completely. Creatinine 81 (18/01/2016)
3. Delayed diagnosis lumbar suburban haematoma, largest at L4 and widening of intervertebral discs at L1–2 and L2–3. Underwent L1–L4 stabilisation under the care of the Consultant Spinal Surgeon. A lumbar drain was inserted and removed and routine post-operative XRs were unremarkable.
4. Acute subarachnoid haemorrhage. Mr Izadi was monitored with regards to his left subdural haematoma. A routine follow-up CT Head on 30/12/2015 showed trace acute

subarachnoid haemorrhage within the precentral sulcus at the vertex and there is also a very small volume of dependent acute blood within the lateral ventricles. This finding was despite Mr Izadi having not had further trauma or anticoagulation. This was discussed with neurosurgery, however it was deemed not for surgical intervention, and required follow-up in clinic only. He has subsequently received treatment dose anticoagulation for his pelvic fracture with no complications.

5. Raised ALP. An ultrasound abdomen was performed which showed unremarkable appearance of the liver. Small gallstone notes. No complications. Right kidney demonstrates normal corticomedullary differentiation and cortical thickness and measures approximately 11.5 cm. The left kidney is atrophic and measures 6.4 cm. No hydronephrosis.

6. Right vocal cord palsy. An ENT review was sought as Mr Izadi complained of hoarseness of his voice since his RTA. FNE revealed right vocal cord palsy. Posterior pharyngeal projection due to underlying osteophytic changes of the C3–C4 cervical bodies. There was no intrathoracic cause for his vocal cord palsy therefore he has been commenced on thickened fluids until SLT assessment (which may occur at SMH or Farm Lane).

What had been life-threatening in reality looked almost perfunctory on paper. My body had taken a battering but I had survived and at least I now felt that I was beginning to make some progress.

Back Home
– *Sheida* –

When Mahmoud came home he was in a terrible condition. His legs were swelling up, he couldn't breathe, he couldn't think and he would fall all the time. Even when he didn't fall it was a terrible situation. In our home there were three steps going down from our open-plan kitchen to the living room. If he tried to walk down the steps he would invariably fall over. So a special chair was brought in for him to sit on and he would sit there the whole day. By now we had physios and carers coming around the clock and he would just sit there waiting for each one to arrive. It was very depressing for him. He was given another blood test and they discovered that there was a problem with the medication for his diabetes. Another warning were his legs which were red and swollen. It was due to his heart and kidney problems.

And so he was having good days and then bad ones but there was no particular pattern to them. On one of the bad ones I woke up at two o'clock one morning to find him getting dressed.

'What are you doing?' I asked him.

'Getting ready to go to the office,' he replied.

'Get undressed and come back to bed,' I instructed, concerned that although things had got better in some ways, he was still obviously confused about things in many others. It was not the first time that this had happened and I knew that we couldn't go on like this much longer. His voice was still very soft, his eyes were bad and he was still struggling to walk. And it seemed as though we had a constant stream of carers, nurses and physios coming in and out of our home at all times of the day. It had begun to feel very intrusive. I felt like I had no privacy anymore and it was driving me crazy. And the worst part was that it had been going on for months and there didn't seem to be an end to it anytime soon. In addition to the rehab and having to cope with emergency visits to hospital, we were also having disagreements as well. I could sense his frustration with everything that was or wasn't happening. His frustrations weren't helping me much either. By now I was close to breaking point and was getting quite desperate. I would actually punch the wall whilst I was crying. It was almost as though I had to do something physical to relieve the mental pressure. Mahmoud had been through so much of course, but I had too and when he had left the hospital and then rehab it was left to me to pick up the pieces. So I called our GP and explained the situation. Mahmoud couldn't visit the surgery because he couldn't walk down the steps that led to it and so the GP came to visit us at home. I talked to her about my own situation as well as Mahmoud's loss of short-term memory, the confusion around it and having to deal with it all on a day to day basis.

Mahmoud had lost the strength in his legs and had been discharged from rehab too early. This led to all sorts of problems, one of which was that he just kept falling over. He was using a walker for balance but he still wasn't that stable. So every time he lost control at home and I was near him I would put my knees in front of him to help him avoid falling. But what would happen is that he would fall on top of me. It was actually then really difficult for us to get back up to our feet. I would turn him over and would have to try and pull myself up using whatever was to hand for leverage. I would then call for an ambulance and they would have to come and check to see if we were okay. It happened four times and it was very frustrating as well as uncomfortable. Although with every new occurrence the whole situation actually became quite farcical and I began to see the funny side of it all. In some way it was a light-hearted moment in a period of darkness.

But one good thing was that he was having regular scans and it showed that the blood clot was shrinking in size. Mahmoud's memory was also getting a little better but it felt like a very long process.

I had been through hell for two years but I knew that talking to God would help me. I asked him for the strength to be able to cope with this difficult situation and find a way forwards. Somehow I found the strength to do so. I knew that Mahmoud couldn't cope alone and I prayed to God that he would get better. His predicament was now affecting both our lives.

I said to him not to forget that God had given him another life and how I had used the Koran and my faith to help him whilst he was in the hospital. He said of course and showed respect but deep down I don't think he really believed in the sense of the religious book.

He then began to tell me about his experience in the other world. His memories were so vivid and he was so clear as to what had happened. It was a world away from what he was experiencing now in terms of clarity and I believed in what he was saying. He told me that there must be a reason for him to stay alive, but that he didn't know yet what it was.

Learning to Walk

I was trying to weigh up everything that had happened to me whilst learning to keep my balance and not fall over as I took my first tentative steps of the day unaided. On this particular morning my head was winning and my legs were losing. It was very frustrating. But the thoughts in my head were not always consistent. I couldn't say for sure that I remembered all the things that were happening even when I left St Mary's Hospital and started my rehab. It was all a bit of blur and was a mixture of recollections and what Sheida and various other people had told me. I sometimes found it difficult to remember something that happened the day before but then could remember an event from many years ago.

Physically, things had improved when I started my physiotherapy in rehab. I had begun to walk again and regaining some sort of physicality helped me back into the real world. I did have vague recollections of my two great friends Shabaz and Mehrdad visiting me but I couldn't pinpoint exact times or dates. I was unbelievably grateful for their support but I couldn't tell you any real specifics about what we talked about. But what I did remember, with an amazing degree of clarity, was my experience in the other world. I had begun to tell Sheida about my incredible experiences and my recollections about my time there were just so vivid as well as extraordinary.

But right now I was concentrating on learning to walk again. Sheida thought that I had been released too early from rehab because I wasn't really capable of the physical management of my life. But here I was and I was determined to make the best of it. I was assigned physiotherapy for home visits. My supervisor was a lovely New Zealand girl called Melinda. She would come to visit me twice a week and walk me slowly up and down the corridor in my home. The physiotherapy treatment progressed and she would take me out in the street to get a taste of a new environment. We used to do about three or four hundred yards before heading back to where we lived. Slowly, slowly, I began to get my legs back.

But in the meantime, I was falling down a lot when other people weren't around and sometimes even when they were too. Some of the falls would be quite nasty and I cut my head open on several occasions when I just went straight down without warning. But it didn't put me off. Even though there were times when I really struggled, I would come back to it, day after day. One major problem that I had was the fact that once I had actually fallen over, I was often too weak to get up again. The carers would have to come in and help me. It was very disconcerting and it seemed strange as my legs were getting stronger. I didn't know why it was happening. None of the doctors seemed to know either. But because of my past history, if I was outside when I fell, an ambulance would be called. They would examine me in the back of the ambulance and because they didn't want to take any risk with concussion, I would be rushed into the Chelsea and Westminster Hospital. This would happen over and over and it was incredibly frustrating. Eventually the doctors discovered that the problem was that my heart was in such a terrible condition that I wasn't getting enough blood to the muscles in my legs. But I carried on with the physio as I was so determined to make some progress and get better. I had a panic alarm that I used to wear around my neck, but as is so often the way with these things, it was one of the few times that I wasn't wearing it that something happened.

On that particular day I became unsteady on my feet and fell over in the bathroom. I couldn't move and without the panic alarm had no way to communicate with anyone. Sheida was staying with Samira for a few days and so I was on my own. I tried as hard as I could to move but I just didn't have the strength to do it. And then I started to get concerned. I had managed to overcome so many difficulties: the impact of the accident, the lung problem, the blood clot on my brain, the breathing difficulties, being in the coma, the spine operation, getting septicaemia three times and now here I was just lying on my bathroom floor. I was effectively helpless. I didn't know what to do and things were getting pretty serious. I couldn't see how I would get out of the situation. I really was on my own because the carers were no longer coming in every day. But then I heard my phone ringing in another room. I couldn't get to it to answer it of course and so whoever it was who was trying to get hold of me was out of luck. The phone rang off. But then a few moments later it rang again. And then again. This pattern repeated itself over the next three hours and it was unbelievably frustrating not being able to move or get to the phone. But the fact that whoever was calling me kept on trying, gave me hope. And then a short while later, it stopped ringing. I just lay there, unsure of what I could do anymore. And at that point I wondered if this was finally it and that all my struggles had been in vain.

But then the next thing I knew, the front door suddenly opened and the emergency services appeared in my bathroom and rescued me. They had used a key left for the carers to let themselves in. My daughter Nilu had been making the phone calls and trying to get hold of me. When she hadn't got a reply, after a while she had become really worried and contacted the emergency services. I was extremely grateful that she had done so.

The days went by and the physiotherapy continued as did my attempts to keep walking. Falls became an occupational hazard if not a particularly nice one. And then one day I had another fall when I went out to do some shopping.

It was at the same Tesco's where I had been struck by the SUV! The incident wasn't quite as dramatic as before but it was still a bit of a shock. One minute I was doing my shopping and the next minute I was flat on my face. After another hospital visit and more tests, the doctors concluded that what I needed was a pacemaker. And so that's what they gave me.

I had been through hell and high water with all the falls. I was always *afraid* that I was going to fall which was almost as bad as actually falling. But once my pacemaker had been fitted, it did its job controlling my heart and blood supply and I didn't fall again. But I had other issues to contend with. I was now having conflicts with Sheida. All marriages have their moments, but things were difficult between us and it resulted in quite a lot of stress and anxiety. With my ongoing medical condition not helping matters, there were times where I yearned just to be back in the other world. I was much younger in that world. And the weather, the scenery, the beautiful house I had in Tehran, all my friends, the colours and the total lack of any problems or aggravation meant that I was always on cloud nine. It really was a magnificent world. I was curious and anxious but I was happy. I knew that nothing could happen to me there. In the other world, I was in heaven.

Breaking Point
- Sheida -

I was trying to do everything I could to help Mahmoud. He had made great improvements in many ways. His long-term memory was fine and he remembered things about his childhood and stories about his friends and family. But his short-term memory was gone. He was confused and irrational and then aggressive and depressed. He continued his physical rehab with an iron will, but he would keep on falling over and he was constantly having to go in and out of hospital. I was worried about his behaviour and that he might hurt himself again. It was both scary and exhausting and I realised that I couldn't live with it.

When Mahmoud had been in hospital I had enlisted the prayers of all my cousins. They had all been fantastic but one of them had been particularly supportive. Her name was Mashid and she was a Muslim who did a lot of Sufi gatherings. She had already spoken to Mahmoud and sent him a lot of energy by telephone.

Mahmoud was sleeping a lot during the day and she sent him some prayers on audio and video and I would place a device by his ears so that he could listen to them. The prayers gave the body energy overall and then depending on where the device was placed it would give energy to specific places such as his head to repair the blood clot. Everyone was doing their best to help Mahmoud and although he was much better he was not always alert. But Mashid spoke to him on the phone again and told him that she was forwarding these videos of people praying and singing in this Sufi style. She was convinced it would help him.

But although we were all helping Mahmoud, I really needed help too. I had reached breaking point. The stress had finally got to me and I knew that I had to do something about it. The main issue was my lack of sleep. It was beginning to really affect me and I was starting to have more and more morbid thoughts. What would happen to Mahmoud if he died? Would he want to be buried or cremated? We had never discussed such things.

I was never a very good sleeper anyway. And I knew lack of sleep would kill me unless I addressed it properly. I had started taking sleeping pills from the day that I arrived back in London and realised that Mahmoud was in such bad shape. I wanted nothing more than for Mahmoud to get better and feel better about himself. But although things had calmed down he was clearly still not okay. I was trying my best to do the right thing but the emotional strain of looking after Mahmoud and dealing with all the other stuff that was going on around us was enormous. And the day to day living in our domestic situation was getting almost impossible. I could hardly eat, had lost 4 kg in weight and was having trouble sleeping.

It was all getting too much. Months and months of stress had been building up and I felt like it would never end. When one problem was overcome, another one would replace it almost immediately. Mahmoud had come home but was spending half the time going back into hospital if he had a fall or a complication. I could barely cope with it all. It was a different kind of pressure to when I was having to go to the hospital every day, but in its own way it was just bad. I had only been able to get this far because of the kindness of my daughter and grandchildren. I was able to stay with them because I was so scared at what might happen. I knew couldn't afford to get seriously ill. But enough was enough.

I called my cardiologist and told him that I wasn't feeling well. I had already had a stent inserted for issues with my heart and it should have been doing its job. But with all the stress and running around trying to sort out everything I was only getting three or four hours sleep every night which wasn't enough. I was taking sleeping pills which could give you eight hours sleep, but I was also worried about taking them the whole time as they were very addictive. After speaking to my cardiologist, I then admitted myself to the Royal Brompton Hospital in Sydney St. My cardiologist did a few tests and then told me that the stent for my heart was not working properly and was 'clogged up'. They decided to perform an angioplasty which meant inserting another stent under local anaesthetic.

After the procedure they took me upstairs to recover. So there I was in the Royal Brompton Hospital recovering from an operation and not far away Mahmoud was in the Chelsea and Westminster recovering from one of his many setbacks. He had been in and out of there so many times it was becoming his second home. I decided to Skype him.

I told him what had happened but that it had all gone well and that I was now okay. We each listened as the other one went through their own events of the day. We had both been through so much in our own ways that it was almost fitting that we were both talking whilst lying on hospital beds! Despite everything I had a sense of relief now and I was feeling quite calm. I felt that there was a way forward and I could already feel the stress lifting off me. The scenario was actually quite amusing, because although we were both in different hospitals we were both wearing matching white gowns with blue dots. As we chatted away to each other in this slightly surreal situation we made quite the picture.

Back to Tehran

It was now late October 2017. I had continued to make steady progress on all fronts concerning my injuries. The doctors had finally decided to put me on medication that would dry the blood clot on my brain but not cause any serious side effects that might lead to damage later on. It seemed to work and my head injury was slowly getting better.

I still couldn't walk unaided for any great distance, although I could now make it to about thirty or forty yards before I became unstable. The damage in my left eye had resulted in water behind the retina. The doctors and specialists had tried everything to cure it and now thought that laser treatment might work. I was undergoing my rehab by doing exercises in a swimming pool to help my legs and I was determined to walk unaided again.

My life had been built around my love of meeting people and social interaction. So when I had come out of the coma having lost my voice, it was a real blow. My vocal chords had been damaged because of the tube – which of course helped stabilise my breathing – but I could barely talk in more than a whisper and I found it very frustrating. When I had first seen my cousin Nasser in London after coming out of hospital, he had hardly been able to hear a word that I was saying.

There were more frustrations. I had always loved singing and used to sing Frank Sinatra and Nat King Cole songs, but I couldn't get a tone out of my mouth. Even worse, my grandchildren were now afraid of the way I talked. It was too gruff and my voice was too inconsistent and they didn't like it. As a result they started avoiding me. Even Sheida would occasionally ask what was happening with my voice.

And to add to all this frustration I had tried to see a voice specialist for some time, but for some reason although my doctor kept on referring me, I had not got a response. But eventually I did get a response from St Mary's Hospital and I went there and tested my voice. I was referred to a voice trainer, Nicola Craven, at the Chelsea and Westminster Hospital.

She told me that it had all been a bureaucratic balls-up and I should have been able to see her a long time before I did. But then she started the voice training and it began to work wonders. The tube had damaged and paralysed my left vocal cord. What the voice training did was try and activate and move the cord, so that when I talked the two vocal cords coordinated together. The physical impairment was one element, but it also affected the mental side as well.

My voice had always been a huge part of who I was as a person. I used to love telling jokes and imitating my favourite singers. I used to sing at parties. Janeau and I used to sing together at parties. It was a fun part of my life. Having my voice back now helped me on many levels. Not just the ability to speak properly again and be heard, but getting compliments on something that had gone well made me feel more complete as a person. It made me feel that anything was possible. So physically and mentally I was in a much better place than I had been in for a long, long time. But spiritually I still had things that I needed to resolve.

Now I had some of my strength back, Sheida and I had decided to visit Tehran and some of the cousins who had been so supportive with their prayers and positive energy. I wasn't sure whether I was looking forward to seeing the city again with all its changes. But I knew that it would be a lot better than the first time I had gone back since the revolution. That had been a nerve-wracking experience.

In 1994, I had been scared of returning to Tehran because of my relationship with the Shah's royal family and the fact that there was a purge against people like me. Not to mention that my ex-father-in-law was the head of the oil company and a man with much influence in the corridors of power. But having weighed up the pros and cons I decided to risk it and go back.

I was nervous the whole flight over but there was to be no turning back. I was travelling with my girlfriend and as I entered passport control and handed over my passport for scrutiny I really had no idea as to what would happen next. The official took one look at it, made a note and the next thing I knew I was being sent upstairs for an interview and further questioning. I was bloody terrified. I was told by an official not to worry because everybody who had been away from the country for a long time, such as I had been, went through the same process. I didn't believe him for a second. They asked me hundreds of questions and I began to be increasingly worried as to what this was all leading to. Finally, after about five hours of questioning they let me go. But they kept hold of my passport. I almost had a heart attack. With my passport now invalidated I was powerless and couldn't leave the country.

I spent the next month in Iran not hearing anything and I constantly worried about what they might do or not do and whether worse was to come. It was incredibly stressful. I had built up an amazing life for myself in England, but once I had made the decision to come back to Iran I knew that I had to go through with it and if there was going to be a problem that I had to face it head on. It was what I always did in my life. The waiting and tension continued until, after six weeks, I heard that I had been deemed to have 'cleared my name'.

I had been incredibly lucky. The officials who had first interviewed me had made no mention of my past royal connections with the Shah. I had no idea of how I would be treated, but they had taken me at face value and judged me on the person that had stood in front of them. It was a great relief and at long last, I was officially given an approval letter that allowed me to get my new passport. Although I wasn't a government official of the previous regime, I could have been shoved into jail or even executed. I hadn't been able to say for sure what would happen when I had come back to Iran and I had other friends with past royal connections who had not been as fortunate as me.

As I came back to Tehran this time with Sheida, I still had certain feelings about both the people and the country itself. But living in London I also had the benefit of perspective. At root level Iranians in London were no different to those in Tehran. But some of them had a misconception about going back to Iran. They detested the mullahs and they thought that the country was still oppressed. They thought that they were in danger. They wanted to remember Iran the way that they knew it. That applied to a lot of my friends too, but deep down I knew that a lot of them would like to go back to their homeland.

Before the revolution Tehran had had all these beautiful tree-lined avenues but they had all now become part of the new urban development. On one particular day, I had lunch with a dear old friend of mine and when you looked out of his garden you could almost see the area in which we all had lived. But the gardens and houses were all high-rises now and I just didn't want to know. I wanted to remember it the way it was. But as the saying goes, nothing stays the same forever.

The changes to the skyline and city infrastructure had another knock-on effect. It meant that I didn't know where I was in Tehran anymore. Mount Damavand, which as a boy I had used as a reference point in the city, was now obscured by the city smog. I had learnt the city's streets and had known where each specific street would take me, be it to a family member's house, to friends, or to an oil company I would do business with. But those streets didn't exist anymore and had been replaced by tunnels and bridges as part of the urban development. I couldn't relate to them at all. I was often amazed when I was told by someone where we actually were, as it all seemed so alien to me. I had now become more familiar with London than Tehran, mainly due to the fact that the layout of the city didn't change.

But if Tehran had changed the people hadn't changed. No matter what regime runs Iran you can't get rid of the secularism of Iranian characters. They are tolerant and will abide, but will also go on with their lives and have all their parties. Nothing changes, the Iranian will never change. They always go back to their roots and they still have their sense of humour and their mannerisms. When I went out in the markets and bazaars, if I tried to buy something I would say to the seller, 'How much?' and they would reply, 'Don't mention it, it's yours.' Of course they didn't mean it, but that's what they said. They were too embarrassed to tell you and then of course they would tell you. You couldn't get rid of that lovely secularism of the Iranians. And I loved that about them.

But aside from indulging in the city's general nostalgia, I also had a specific goal when I was out there. My father's hotel had been unlawfully taken during the Iranian revolution and from London I had contacted this very important person who was trying to get it back for me. Unfortunately he had not been able to do so and I had introduced another man to him to act as a liaison, or a man on the ground as it were, whilst I was still in London. A flurry of emails had gone back and forth between us about what he was doing and how he was helping make real progress. I was excited and thought that at last I was getting somewhere.

We arranged to meet up on my visit to discuss how things were going. But when I arrived in Tehran he made every excuse under the sun not to meet me. I wasn't sure what was happening at first, but finally I met up with the initial contact who told me the whole story. Rather than helping me, the liaison had in fact used my introduction to leverage a position with my contact and was now in fact working for him instead on an unrelated project. I was shocked and felt totally betrayed. Of course when word got back to the liaison he sent me a grovelling email, apologising for what had happened and trying to make things work again. But by then it was far too late and I dismissed it.

My greatest weakness is that I'm gullible. When I listen to people I find it difficult to judge a true character. I always look for the best in people and give them the benefit of the doubt. And God knows how many of them have disappointed me as a result. The world has changed and not for the better in this respect. I used to do business on a trust basis and seal it with a handshake. This worked for many years. But now I count my fingers after every handshake instead.

But the best thing about the whole trip was the fact that Sheida was there with me. It was great for us both to get out of London and travelling together made the whole experience far more enjoyable. I was lucky enough to get to know Sheida's extended family and stay with them in Tehran. I met Sheida's cousin, Minoo, a world authority on AIDS and infectious diseases as well as her husband Koroush, a general surgeon and MD of the biggest hospital in Iran. They had both helped Sheida enormously whilst I was in hospital both in terms of practical advice and general support.

And then we met up with Mashid, another of Sheida's cousins who was an intellectual and a Sufi, adhering to an ancient form of Islamic mysticism. She claimed that she had saved my life! I knew that she had recited a special verse to me on the phone from Tehran when I was in hospital and that she had sent me spiritual vibrations. An amazing person she was a lot of fun to be around. On one occasion we attended a party and as usual I was using my walking stick as an aid. I was keen to know when the card game started and so asked Mashid if she knew when that was.

'Well darling, if you start moving now, by the time you get there we will have served dinner,' she replied. We began playing an Iranian card game Pasoor and as the evening progressed I found I was playing quite well. 'My God, you've improved,' she said. 'I think when you had your accident your brain was rewired.' Having been through so much, being around the right people meant so much to me now, especially those who looked for the positive things in life. They inspired me. But they weren't only the inspirational discoveries on the trip.

A trip to the Golestan Palace museum was proposed and we decided to pay it a visit. Set in beautiful gardens it was the royal residence and governing base of the Qajar ruling family during the dynasty's rule of Iran. It was my ancestral home and contained fabulous mosaics and ornate art and sculptures. Amongst them was an extraordinary piece of my family history. My great grandfather, Naser-Din Shah, had been buried in the Shah Abdol Azim shrine. A magnificent marble tombstone marked his grave and during the Islamic revolution, the tombstone was misplaced and so to stop it being desecrated it was brought to the Golestan Palace. Renowned as a magnificent piece of sculpture it bore his full effigy.

As I stood by his tombstone I reflected upon the fact that I came from one of the largest and most distinguished families in Iran but had now just an elderly aunt, Azar, left in Tehran. I had thirty cousins scattered all over the world but other than my closest cousin Nasser, had no communication with any of them. But here, in the Golestan Palace was one of my ancestors, an Iranian Shah, and it made me so proud of my heritage. I thought of the other world that I had visited and said to myself that the next time I ascended I would see all of my ancestors. Whilst I was there I also reflected on how things had changed for myself. I was so grateful to my wife, Sheida, for many things, but to discover her wonderful family and the kindness and charm of her relatives was simply amazing. It negated what I had lost.

The trip was a great success and it was really uplifting meeting such fascinating people. It gave me great energy and a new lease of life. Seeing my great grandfather's tombstone and meeting Sheida's family with their strong spiritual beliefs, inspired me to redouble my efforts about my own beliefs and I vowed that when I got back to London I would go a little deeper in my quest to answer some of the questions that I still had on my mind.

Spiritual Fulfilment

Just before Christmas 2017 I had the breakthrough that I was looking for and that put everything else into perspective. My time in the other world had been eye-opening and I had total clarity about the actual experience. But I still wasn't totally at peace with myself and I needed to find out what it all meant. With Sheida's help I had looked into the Islamic faith in greater detail and I had read various books on the subject by Islamic scholars such as Karen Armstrong and Reza Aslan. Having read these books I saw another aspect of the Islamic religion. But I still had more questions and the truth was that I hadn't yet found satisfactory answers. I had spent almost two years struggling with lots of physical and mental issues and I knew there was something more out there and that I needed to discover it. So I decided to go back to the Brompton Oratory where I had experienced such a strong and powerful spiritual moment before my accident.

I approached the church along the Brompton Rd. With its striking neoclassical architecture, the church was a Grade II listed building and its imposing presence added a sense of importance to my mission the nearer I got to it. But when I arrived at the church entrance I was in for a shock. The large wooden doors at the entrance were shut. It was closed. I managed to find out that a private service was taking place and the church was not open to members of the public. So I gave it a few days and then tried once more. But it was to no avail. It was closed again, but this time I wasn't sure why. I couldn't believe it. Having had my experience entering the other world,

I found it quite hard to take that I wasn't able to enter into a church in this world!

I needed a new plan and then I remembered that there was another church quite near me in West London. It also happened to be a Roman Catholic church but that was incidental as far as I was concerned. I just wanted to experience the feeling that I had experienced before. I set off the next day and as I neared my newly chosen church my hopes soared. But once inside I knew immediately that there was no atmosphere. It felt cold and I didn't like it. I tried to pray but I couldn't find the words. So instead I changed tack. Normally when I went to church, I would always light candles for my mother and father and I could see that it was possible to do so here. But then I realised that in this church you had to pay to light the candles. It just didn't feel right and I felt deflated about the whole thing. Having had enough I decided to leave and on the way back I noticed a homeless man selling the *Big Issue* outside a supermarket. Feeling for him, I gave him my 'church candle money' instead.

I started to question what was going on. It seemed like I wasn't having any success with these churches and I wondered whether I was doing the right thing. I started to think about all the religious experiences that I had been through in my life before visiting the other world.

As a boy, I had been brought up in an atmosphere in Tehran where all my grandparents, uncles and aunts prayed every day. There were religious ceremonies in the streets where people used to flagellate themselves on the days when the Imams were martyred. It didn't affect my parents as they took it for granted but it definitely affected me as a child. I thought it was a horrible, frightening sight. People would draw blood by hitting themselves with sharp objects and they would beat themselves on the chest. They thought that if they hit themselves hard enough they would die and then go to heaven. I found the severity of it both frightening and abhorrent. It seemed like it was fanatical. It terrified me and made me terrified of religion.

When I had come to England and gone to school at Langley, what had terrified me at that age were the graveyards and gravestones. But at Langley there was also a beautiful, old chapel. And when I became a prefect at the age of sixteen I used to stand in the chapel and read the Christian lessons. It was lovely and as far as I was concerned the Protestant faith was a religion of love. By going to chapel at Langley I became less and less frightened of religion. Christianity seemed like a religion of love and forgiveness as opposed to one of the sword and blood.

At Cambridge I was scientist, rationalising what I was learning about evolution and my thoughts turned away from religion. I didn't have much time for it.

When my parents were living in London I had confronted them with my views on some of the more fanatical aspects of their faith. My father had mellowed considerably by then and agreed with some of my points of view, but my mother was afraid of offending her faith and it was too late in her life for her to want to change.

My father and I had actually shared a formative religious experience many years before. I was working for H&G at the time and had to go to Baghdad on business. We had just bought a Mercedes to take to Tehran and he suggested that instead of shipping the car we could drive it over from Iraq via Europe. Iraq is known as the Mecca of all Shi'ite prophets. Ali was the son-in law of Muhammad. His two sons Hasan and Husayn are buried there. They are all martyred. My father was a devoutly religious man and wanted to make the pilgrimage there via a road trip that started in Europe but finished in the Middle East. I agreed to do it and we set off on our adventure from London. We travelled through France and Switzerland into Italy until we reached the port of Naples. We took the boat to Beirut and from there drove to Jordan and Iraq. I needed to go to my meeting but my father wanted to stop at Karbala, a holy city in Iraq where all the prophets are buried. We visited Karbala and went to the tombs of the Imams. My father was in his element, praying and crying. I didn't feel quite so moved by it all until I visited the tomb of Imam Ali I and I was gripped by an almost electrical spiritualism. It was mesmerising and I couldn't leave the tomb for ages. It was the first deep spiritual feeling that I had ever had in my life.

I had also visited Mecca and had gone around the Kaaba, but it was a different kind of experience and although I had a strong sense of fulfilment, I didn't have the same explosion of spirituality as in Karbala.

I still didn't have the clear answers I was looking for. I resolved to try the Brompton Oratory once more and see if I could actually get inside this time. I wanted to see if it was as spiritual as I remembered and I knew that I wouldn't be satisfied until I found out.

I arrived at the church with some trepidation that I wouldn't be able to get in. But this time I just walked through the open doors. The interior was full of splendour as I remembered it and as I walked to the front pews I felt the same emotional pull as before. It felt just right and the atmosphere was calm and peaceful. I sat in the same place that I had sat in before my accident and looked up at the prominent cross up above me.

A feeling of spirituality just flooded through me and I had this incredible spiritual vibration to the soul. And then I confronted God with my questions.

'What did you do to me? What happened? What's the message in all this?' I asked him. I needed to know the answers. 'Why am I here? I should be dead. I only had a 7% chance of survival. Why did you send me back here again? Am I to achieve some incredible thing in my life that would benefit mankind?' I continued on, 'Bless my daughter and my wife. Bless my mother and father. And thank you for your providence.'

I wasn't expecting immediate answers but even just asking the questions made me incredibly fulfilled. I now believed that I had found my true spirituality and I came out of the church with a feeling of incredible spiritual strength. I was hoping to find peace and solace and I had come out enriched with something divine. It felt like I had discovered something within me, my true spirituality. For some reason I had needed to have an accident, survive my injuries and visit the other world in order to make me realise how powerful my own spirituality really could be.

I was just so glad that I had finally made it to the church because I hadn't been there since I had come round from my coma. The last two years quickly came into focus. I shouldn't have made it back from my injuries. They were catastrophic and I knew that nobody really thought that I would survive. But something deep inside of me would not give in. And now I was having this incredible spiritual moment where at last I could feel that my dark skies of despair were lifting and beginning to disappear.

I hadn't gone to the Brompton Oratory because of its church denomination. I had gone there because it was a place of God and I happened to feel deeply spiritual in that place. As far as I was concerned I had felt a true spiritual connection with my God and was speaking to him whilst I was in there. It just happened to be in that particular place of worship. The fact that the church was of a Roman Catholic denomination did not sanctify the experience for me. How could it? My parents were of Islamic faith and I already knew that I was going to see them again. I had embraced a multitude of different faiths and religions before in my life, but now I had experienced a new spiritual awakening and it wasn't connected to any particular faith. It was my own belief and my religion was a nucleus which is God.

Hope

The Florida warmth was the perfect place to continue my ongoing rehab and my voice was definitely improving. I was swimming for about forty minutes every day and I was trying everything I could in terms of mobility to help my legs. I was pedalling, creating leg movements and back movements. I wanted to go to the tennis court and let alone play tennis, just volley at the net. But I was too unstable even to do that. I wasn't sure that I would ever play tennis again and I thought that I would be walking around with a stick for the rest of my life. I had tried everything that I could think of in terms of trying to get full use of my legs again. None of it had really worked so far. But I would never give up trying to find another solution.

I had always loved the challenge of what life throws at you and not knowing what might happen next. It was part of the reason that I liked meeting new people. You never knew what might come out of it. I suppose that as much as anything people liked me for the fact that I treated everyone the same way no matter who they were.

In my working life I had met some of the most powerful people in the world, including business leaders, presidents and kings. Sometimes, I did think to myself that if there was one thing that I wished I had done differently, it would have been to utilise my situation to better effect. People used to invite me to events and social occasions because they thought I was fun and cultured. I can't explain why, but I found it very easy to make friends quickly. I was very humble towards the great figures that I met, but the truth is that I was just being myself.

This easy camaraderie took place on many occasions and one of them was when I met King Hussein of Jordan. I met him at a cocktail party at the Dorchester Hotel. We chatted and laughed for about an hour. I can't tell you exactly what I said to him, but whatever it was it must have made an impression because the next day I received a message from the Jordanian embassy in London. They had got my name from the host of the party – it wasn't too difficult as I had been the only Iranian there – and the message said that the King would like to see me for dinner. Sadly, diary conflicts prevented it from happening, but instead I received an open invitation to visit him in Jordan at any time and to please contact him. I should have taken have him up on his offer.

It was example of how easy I found it to talk to anyone. But deep down I knew that I could and should have made more of the opportunity. It was just one of those things. Little did I know that over the next few days a remarkable opportunity to utilise my talents would present itself in a way that I could never have imagined.

I had been through an extraordinary experience which had helped me discover my true spirituality. And now I felt at peace both with myself and the world around me. But there was still one question that lingered in my mind. I was seventy-nine years old and had led a very full life. So what was my purpose now? I had asked God the question in the church and despite my joy embracing a new-found spirituality, I hadn't yet found the answer. But that was all about to change.

Sheida and I flew to Houston to see her brother, Shahin and whilst we were there we were invited out to a local restaurant by her brother-in-law Jimy. It was a lovely, casual affair where we ate at the bar. We were introduced to a delightful couple that we had never met before and as we all sat down I couldn't help noticing that the husband looked a little shaky. I didn't think much more of it and the evening continued. As is the way on these occasions we exchanged a few stories and then Sheida's brother-in-law told the couple that I had been in a very serious accident. They seemed keen to hear all about it. So I duly told them all about the accident and the coma and then went on to mention that I had gone to another world, to paradise, and then what had happened when I saw my four deceased friends. And all of a sudden the husband just lit up with excitement. He wanted to know more and more details and so I told him everything that I could about the experience. Later on in the evening, his wife took me to one side.

'You don't know what you've done for him,' she said to me. She then proceeded to tell me how he was suffering from MS and that he was incredibly worried about what would happen to him in the future. Until, that is, I told him my story.

And then a few days later Sheida and I travelled to Miami to visit a friend and soon after met her brother-in-law. He was a very successful businessman and we got chatting and once more my story became a topic of conversation. He had known my friend Parviz Radji and wanted to know more about the accident, so again I told him about it as I had done with the other couple in Houston.

I noticed that he was gawking at me as I spoke and before long he bombarded me with a whole series of questions. Everything from where I had been, to where I had slept, to where I went and so on and so forth. I told him that I had been in my house on Ehteshamiyeh Avenue. My food had been prepared, the garden, the swimming pool, everything was pristine and looked after. He kept on asking me every question under the sun. Once again, later on that evening I discovered that he was suffering with an illness and had been feeling unsure and worried about his situation but that by speaking to me and hearing my story, he had found a certain peacefulness.

And that's when I realised what my purpose was. I knew why I had come back to this world and what God wanted me to do. When I had found my spirituality, I still hadn't really known. But having these two conversations with two people that I had never met before clarified everything.

Quite simply, I was here to give people who were suffering hope that there was a better place to go to. I hadn't known that those two people were both suffering, if not dying, but I knew that throughout their lives people needed hope to go forwards in life and that at the end of one's life it could be very scary and difficult to find such a positive message.

I wasn't going to preach about my experience but I was now in the position to help others like never before. And I wanted to be able to make them understand that in times of immense stress at the end of your life, all was not lost and that there was something to look forward to.

It give me huge satisfaction to realise this as well as the great joy of actually being be able to help others. I was at peace with my mortality and I could give them that hope as well. I had made my peace with the world and God and now I would help others to do the same.

In my Life

The reason that I wrote this book is that my experience in the other world was so overwhelming that I wanted to share it with other people. The clarity of thought, tranquillity and lack of tension that I experienced in that world left an incredible impact on me. I had lamented my close friends for a long time after they had died and just to see them all again and in such great fettle was a source of unbelievable comfort. I now view the everyday problems and challenges that I face in a very different way to how I faced them before. I am so much more understanding now. Whether it's an everyday issue that we all might have – a family disagreement or a misunderstanding between friends – I am much less reactive in the way that I respond. I have become much more philosophical about life and I find it far easier to take things with a pinch of salt. I have realised that when it comes to the people who are in my life, some of them will never change. No matter what I do or say, if they don't actually want to change or are not prepared to try, it won't make any difference. I have come to accept that now and am able to move on with other things in my life. What my experience has given me is a greater clarity of what's really important to me.

When I started writing, it made me feel very happy. Not only was it therapeutic because of what I had just been through, it revived my memories of childhood which are very important to me. I recalled different aspects of my life and it was wonderful remembering the intimacy of my relationships.

One of these was with my daughter Nilu. She was brought up by her mother, but as she grew up, I made sure that I saw her as much as possible. Being my only child she is an amazing part of my life. But I had no idea that the accident would bring her so close to me. She came to me and I welcomed her with open arms. It was wonderful and I realised that my consideration for my daughter has been fulfilled.

What I find extraordinary is that I can remember my journey to heaven so clearly. It was so vivid and I can remember every single detail, every sensory experience. But I don't have any memory of anything leading up to it. I don't remember anything about the accident. I don't remember giving family contact details to the emergency services. I don't remember speaking to Sheida on the phone or Nilu in the hospital. I don't remember seeing any of the consultants who treated me or the nurses who looked after me. And I don't really remember responding to anyone about anything from the moment that I was hit until I came to from my coma.

My experience has had a profound effect on me. I have become calmer and much more philosophical about life. I don't fear mortality in the slightest sense. The only thing I wish is that when my time comes, that it does so quickly. I don't want to go through what my friends went through with all the chemotherapy. I will never have it. I saw what it did to them and then conversely I saw how happy they were when we were together in a heavenly place.

The reason that I made such an incredible recovery was partly due to my faith, belief and energy. I know that somebody up there loves me because the miracle of my accident is actually that I am not a cripple. I was thrown fifteen feet up into the air and could have landed on my head and had permanent brain damage. I could have landed on another part of my body and been paralysed. I was hit by this SUV and broke my back, my hip, my left knee and damaged my brain. I am now half-blind in my left eye. But to me it's a miracle that I came out unscathed. My voice is so much better than it was and continues to improve. I just need a stick to walk with and a bit of treatment on my eye.

So many things could have been much worse but for some reason, they weren't. My ribs damaged my lungs but they could have gone into my heart and it would have needed a major operation. In the end, the rib came up of its own accord. Of course my wife, Sheida, believes she has the answer as to why it got better. Her cousin in Tehran also thinks so too. I just think that I am lucky that things weren't worse. The doctors had given me 7% chance of survival. And to this day I have no idea how I survived. I should have incurred a fatal injury but somehow I didn't. And the injuries healed themselves. I also contracted septicaemia several times and could have died on multiple occasions. When I had one problem I often developed another one which made the first one even more complicated. A good example of that is the multiple operations that I was due to have where each problem kept on getting in the way of another one. Whether it was my ribs and lungs, my blood clot on the brain, my broken back and so on and so forth. The accident and the subsequent injuries that I endured really were horrendous by anyone's standards. So much so, that during one of my numerous follow-up appointments at St Mary's Hospital, one of the young doctors took me to one side.

'You know Mahmoud, you're indestructible. When I saw you after the accident I wouldn't have given you a bloody chance in hell,' he said. He was clearly surprised that I had pulled through.

***

Sheida is absolutely right. It is a miracle that I survived! But I did and when I came back to this world, I couldn't stop thinking about the obvious question. Why had I come back? What was the point of going through all of that at my age? There had to be a purpose for my return. But I had no idea what that was at that time. My good friends the Khonsaris thought that because

I was such a good person in my life, God didn't want me to die. This was very nice to hear, but in my own mind I wanted to find out what my purpose really was.

And gradually, I began to discover some answers. It started with the large gap of time that was missing from life, from my accident to coming out of the coma. I was told what had happened to me during the accident and how I had overcome almost impossible odds just to survive that. I knew how it affected my family and friends and what they had been through, especially whilst I had been in the coma. I know I visited the other world which was a heavenly place and that I found my own true spirituality as a result. But despite all these things I still wasn't sure about the reason why I had returned to this world. It seemed like there had to be more to it than self-interest but I didn't know what it was for a long time. But I also knew that I wouldn't stop searching until I discovered it. And it took me just under two years to do so. One of the things I have learnt through my experience is that nobody can be certain what will happen tomorrow and sure enough I discovered that final answer when I least expected it.

Because of my near death experience, my relationship with God has now changed and is now much stronger than it was before. I now totally believe in God. As a scientist I doubted him. At Cambridge, because I was studying Darwinism I just couldn't believe in him. I denounced him. I think it's what a lot of people go through in life. They go through a doubt period. But now after this experience, I truly believe that there is a creator coordinating this life. Somebody who coordinates everything that we are and what we do. Having been to the hospital incessantly over the last two years I have come to understand in far greater detail how the organs, nerves and systems all fit together in the human body. It's so exact that the human body has to have been formed by something greater than just evolution. It's much greater than that. My mind is made up completely. There is a God and he is definitely a creator. Look at the seasons. The nudity of the trees in the winter and then suddenly blossoming in the spring. There is a God. There is a creator. And I'm a believer.

I'm looking forward to going back to the other world and seeing what my life will be like up there, but doing it when I'm actually expected and not as a gate-crasher. I believe in the divinity of God but it is my God. I am devoid of any fanaticism. I detest organised religion and the rules and the laws which stand completely outside of what religion is supposed to be. Religion is being abused and I detest that as well.

I think religion is a symbol of love and respect for the old power, the almighty. When you become scared and frightened of religion, as prescribed in all those different factions of religion – the Shiites in Iran, the Orthodox Jews, the Orthodox Catholics and so on, it's an invention of their own and it's not a prescribed religion by the prophets. I respect the prophets because they all preach the same thing: love, respect and justice. But organised religion has been distorted – like Catholicism in the 16th and 17th century with its incredible cathedrals and churches and pomp and ceremony. And in the Muslim religion, their weapon is to put fear into the life of their subjects so that they daren't challenge what the leaders say and what they do. Again, it's 'propheteering', it's not religion.

I identify with God, with Christ and Mohammed. I respect all religions but my true conversion was to spirituality. The real problem with religion is not any specific religion itself, but the people who are involved in it. It's the way that they use it. Sadly, I believe people have corrupted and twisted the doctrines of the prophets for their own gains. It also subscribes to the experience of what happened in the other world. It wasn't just a fragment of my imagination it was something real that happened.

I feel the power and the influence that can be bestowed on you whenever you're depressed or down. There is somebody with me. Somebody I can lean on. And I can talk to God anywhere I feel the spiritual connection. It doesn't matter whether it's a mosque, a synagogue or a church. The place of worship is the house of God. It is where I speak to my God.

What I have learnt is this. Don't be afraid. Follow your heart. Follow your wisdom. Follow your conscience. Find your spirituality and follow your own God. But don't be fooled by the all these horrendous laws and regulations which are put in front of you and which just become hurdles. To paraphrase my dear old Cambridge tutor, Mark Pryor, if you are afraid of everything you will fall into the abyss.

**

The first time I went back to my mother's grave after I had been to the other world was quite a surreal experience. In the past I had had quite long conversations there and it was relaxing to be able to speak what was on my mind and share my news with her. But this time I just said, 'Mummy, I'm still here. I'm back.' The plants had grown high all around her grave and I spent some time cutting them all back. I just prayed for her as I used to. And then I told her that I was sorry that I hadn't seen her in heaven but that I hoped that I would one day. I told her that I had been back in my old house in Daroos and that I had looked for her and my father when I was there but that I couldn't find them. I said to her that Foulad had explained to me why I couldn't see her again and it was obviously because I jumped the gun and went up there before my time.

Before my accident, I used to visit her cemetery on a regular basis but since my experience in the other world, I have found that I don't grieve anymore because to me it's just a matter of time before I join her up there. I saw it all and I was told that I wasn't supposed to be there, but that when the time was right I would be able to see her and my father again. My experience up there was a profound one. But I am no longer afraid and it's really just a question of time before I see all my family again. I saw all my friends and it was so beautiful and so natural, but it wasn't my time.

Going to my mother's grave means something to me now in that it is where her bones are laid. Her spirit is somewhere else and I'm going to join her one day. That emotional feeling about going to her grave has now disappeared because I have found a resolution with my own spirituality.

As far as I'm concerned I'm not apprehensive about anything anymore. There is just no need to be. I have found peace with myself and my God. As a scientist at Cambridge we learnt all aspects of life – everything about the human body as well as the mind. At times you couldn't help but feel that this is all there is. You just come and go, you die and that's it. But it's now a totally different concept as I know that you do go somewhere.

***

I was always gifted and graced by good companions and friends, very good friends. I was the toast of every party and I lived in total luxury until the Iranian revolution came and took away our power base and money and possessions. I feel that in my life I was gifted with a lot of incredible opportunities at Humphrey's and Glasgow and with Derek Lennon to name a few, but what I can't understand is that with all my contacts and all my education, why I never really made it in life like some of other friends did.

But what I can say is that my experience in the other world has completely changed my life. It has taught me that in this world, this is life. This is how it is. This is a life of opportunities and a life of power over the weak. You find very few people that are actually there to help you. It's a jungle basically. To survive in this world you have to be really on your toes and you have to be smart. Life is about what you do with the opportunities that you create. If you don't take them you lag behind, but if you do you get ahead. I feel that I have had success in many ways but with my opportunities, with my background and with my education I shouldn't be worried about anything. I could and should have done much more than I achieved.

But it's also about what's most important to you. It's made me realise how lucky I am to have the great friends and family that I have. Many of my best friends are now gone but I couldn't have asked for better ones than the ones who are still here. The truth is that I am actually embarrassed by my some of my friends' loyalty and unselfishness. I like to think that I reciprocate friendship but the generosity of some of my friends has been extraordinary.

As I grew up, I realised my potential, my education and my heritage because it all became part of my life. I was attracted to the right people at the right time. I always knew which way to go. I knew who to approach and what to say. I learnt the trade very quickly, becoming a director of one of the biggest companies in Britain at a very young age for the time. I enjoyed my life, I worked hard and I knew that I had overcome a lot of obstacles to get to where I was. After visiting the other world, one of the toughest challenges that I faced was all the uncertainties that the real world threw up when I came back. In the other world I had found peace and tranquillity but that wasn't the case here. I found it really difficult trying to adjust to this world, but as I said that is the reality of this life. But I do know that there is somewhere better to go to which gives me great comfort.

***

When I started to remember about my experiences in the other world after I had come out of the coma, I kept it to myself for a while. I knew what had happened but I needed to make some sense of it myself. And I didn't know how other people would react when I told them. Would they think I was going mad? I wasn't really sure how I was going to explain it. It was such a personal experience that I wasn't sure how to talk about it. The first person I told was Sheida but I waited until I was back home. I didn't necessarily have full control over what I was thinking or saying before then anyway. She calmly listened to everything I had to say and then told me that it was the way that I had described my four friends, how they behaved and treated me, that made her think that I had actually been through the experience. It was a relief and made telling everyone else much easier after that.

The experience of going to the other world was unique. I have done many things in this world but there is nothing that I have done that I can compare to that experience. It has led to some incredible insights about my life. I am far more philosophical and much more tolerant than I used to be. I get on much better with my wife than before. She struggles to see why I've changed so much. She can't have an argument with me anymore as I don't rise to things. Life's irritations just don't bother me in the way that they used to.

When I look back at my life it makes me realise what I had and what I have now. The oil industry was part of my life that I have put behind me. No regrets, none whatsoever. The industry has changed as all my contacts have retired or are dead. There is nothing to cling onto. Nothing to reproach. It was a very good life, a very good living and a very good income. I was good at what I did and it was a very interesting life where I saw the world and met some of the most powerful people on the planet.

But because of the time I spent in the other world I have now embraced my God with a new-found spirituality. This makes everything else, all the heartache, all the troubles and all the depressions pale into insignificance by comparison. My fate has meant that I have been lucky enough to experience the highs and lows of one life and have now started a new one with a different but greater meaning.

***

Of course I want the same things that other people want in their life. I want to live long enough to enjoy the growth of my grandchildren and see them go through school. I want my daughter to be happy and I want to make my wife happy. I want Arsenal to continue to win! I want to be able to enjoy all my friends. The usual things that everybody wants. But I would like to offer something else as well.

The experience that I went through was extraordinary. If anyone reading this book wants to know more, I am always available to discuss my spiritual experience and how I formed a relationship with my God. I would be delighted if I can help anyone find their own spirituality in any way.

Since the experience my entire attitude towards life has completely changed. I have become much calmer, much cooler and more realistic. I now feel that spirituality is within me all the time and as a result I just feel protected. I am not scared of anything anymore. I'm not afraid and don't get anxious about all those things that used to worry me.

Finding my spirituality has enabled me to cope with what happened and the physical problems that I have had to endure. I have had a wonderful life, met many fascinating people, visited some amazing countries, made lifelong friends and have an amazing wife and daughter. My life has changed in several ways. Since the accident, although some of my injuries have healed, I can no longer do some of the things that I used to love doing. I can no longer play tennis and for quite a while I did miss being not being able to do that. I missed the camaraderie, the games themselves, the exercise and even the showers afterwards. And sometimes I miss just the pure physicality of exercise. I can't even do the simple things anymore, like run up the steps at the Emirates to watch an Arsenal game. But the truth is that I don't care about those things in the same way that I used to. Sport has played a great part in my life, but in finding my spirituality I have found something that is even greater.

Thank you

My wife, Sheida, is my rock and has always been there for me. She is both an attractive and elegant lady, but at the same time a very smart and tough cookie. She has her beliefs on how I survived my life-threatening injuries and I have mine and we might not agree on everything. But that's okay. Despite all the problems and dramas that we've had to endure, we have somehow come through it all together. I may owe my life to the NHS but I know that I owe everything to her.

My daughter, Nilu, is married and has two wonderful children. I just wish the best for her and her family for the rest of their lives and that no harm comes to them. I never really knew how much my daughter loved me. She kept telling me that she had the greatest admiration for my courage to survive. I just couldn't believe all this love that she showed me and I was embarrassed by her kindness. She's done things and made sacrifices that I can't imagine. They may not be sacrifices to her but they are to me. And strangely, sometimes it's the smallest things that end up meaning the most. For example when I was in rehab at Farm Lane I somehow managed to delete my Sky Go digital app button on my laptop. It was irritating and I mentioned it to Nilu when we were having a conversation on the phone. She was hosting a dinner party for twelve people that night, but she got in her car, drove across London from Peckham to my rehab centre in Fulham, fixed the problem because I didn't know how to do it and then drove back home to continue her evening. Doing that kindness probably didn't mean that much to her, but it meant the world to me.

My brother, Masoud, a retired surgeon, is not an emotional man. But this last Christmas, when he and his and wife came to stay with us in Boca Raton, Florida, I went to meet him at the airport and something incredible happened. We caught sight of each other as he walked through arrivals and as we greeted one another we both burst into tears. It felt like a recognition of hidden closeness which suddenly manifested itself into an emotional outburst when he saw me. And I realised that part of my emptiness has become fulfilled by being with him.

I was really touched. As a younger brother, I had followed in his footsteps since our journey really began all those years ago after being sent to boarding school. He had won the Victor Ludorum as a senior and I won it as a junior. When he left school I took over as the prominent sporting figure and won everything like he had done before me. He got into Durham to study medicine, which in 1953 which was no mean feat because at that time Iran was nationalising it's oil and British universities were not accepting Iranian students.

We spent the week together in Florida and basically solidified what had always been there, but never emotionally demonstrated until this time. He's eighty-one years old and it was just wonderful to be with him and in effect we harmonised our love for each other, which we had always found difficult to do. I'm so glad that we were able to do that. And one day I hope that I am able to do the same with my sister as well. I would also like to thank Samira and Jake for their constant concern about my situation and being a pillar of support towards Sheida.

I realise how lucky I am to have the friends that I have had in my life and how much they mean to me. I don't know what I would have done or where I would now be without them. I am actually embarrassed about how much support Shabaz and Mehrdad showed me when I was in hospital. And of course Nasser and Ghassan have shown me incredible support as well. To me, true friendship means being able to share both happy and sad things with each other. To be able to share views that you are doubtful about because you believe your friends are qualified to give you good advice. Being able to laugh about life together. My friends have been a vital part of my life. After all, what would life be without them?

One of the most important people in my life has been Ghassan Shaker. A longstanding friend, he has the most amazing heart and has shown me incredible kindness and generosity. He is a true gentleman. He basically saved my life. I have known him for the large majority of my life and one of his daughters went to school with my daughter Nilu, when she was at Heathfield.

A highly eminent businessman he is politically connected at the highest possible level. He is incredibly intelligent and knowledgeable regarding political analysis. Prominent in banks, hotels and manufacturing, when it comes to business, you want to be like him.

He has shown me unbelievable support through everything that has happened and I have the utmost respect and love for him. It's difficult to explain our relationship in that we have always had a wonderful camaraderie but at the same time I do know that a line exists and that I won't cross it. We met at Cambridge where I got to know him through Foulad and afterwards we stayed in touch and I saw him in Beirut when he married the prime minister of Lebanon's daughter.

I tried to do business with him both before and after the revolution. Along with Foulad we teamed up with Prince Shahram Pahlavi who was appointed as the agent in Iran for one of our business ventures. The only thing that could stop us was if the Shah was kicked out of Iran. Which unfortunately is exactly what happened. But Ghassan maintained my life standard. Every time I had a potential deal in Oman and Saudi Arabia I would call him. His response was always all encompassing and he would do everything he could do to help the deal go through.

Some of the best relationships are strengthened by little details that to others outside the relationship mean little, if anything at all. My first girlfriend was called Janet and we went out for five years before I got engaged to her whilst I was at Cambridge. One weekend, I was back in Norwich visiting her but I had broken off the engagement. Janet's father, who was a six foot six Norfolk farmer type, took me aside.

'After all's said and done Mahmoud, you've had five years. What are you going to do with her?' he demanded. I told him that I was waiting for my parents to turn up in London but the truth of it was that I was stalling. In my defence, I was still at Cambridge, still quite young and perhaps wasn't quite sure what I wanted out of life or who I wanted in my life.

But the phrase stuck and it has been the calling card between Ghassan and myself for many years. One of those strange little interactions between friends that makes the personal bond between the two of you that little bit stronger.

I knew that Foulad was Ghassan's best friend and that when he died, it devastated him. I was also very close with Foulad and there was a deep connection between the three of us. Despite his great business success and achievement I was always genuine and myself with Ghassan. Without his true friendship I would be at a loss to think what shape my life would have taken after the tragedies of the revolution, the disaster at the restaurant and the devaluation of the Iranian currency. His continued support speaks for itself.

He has always helped me with projects in the Middle East when he has been able to. Hugely influential, his recommendation carries huge weight. Hugely successful, his generosity meant that he would encourage others to share in his success. He used to have this beautiful house in England and would invite two or three hundred people to it every year where they would enjoy food and drink that was without equal. His generosity of spirit extends not just to hosting fantastic parties but helping his friends and those in need. He has been an invaluable person in my life.

I enjoy Shabaz's company because he has a great sense of humour and I connect with him. He went to Oxford, I went to Cambridge. We both went to English boarding schools. We have a lot in common. He's a great tennis player and I was a great tennis player! We enjoy the same attitude towards life, towards everything and everyone. Basically he's the perfect friend.

Mehrdad I've known since he was a child. He used to live opposite our house in Tehran. I didn't know him then but in London we became neighbours in Kensington and then I met him at Queen's. He's a very sharp man who I find extremely intelligent. Of course I don't share all of his political opinions but that's what great friendship is about!

And I must mention my great friend Maan Askari. Our friendship was cemented around sport when we were both at Cambridge. He has been such a wonderful friend over the years and is one of only a few friends still alive from that era. Incredibly well-informed politically he has always liked to do things with a certain style. When I made that incredible road trip with my father, Maan was working for the Iraq Petroleum Company in Kirkuk and arranged for a car to come and collect me when we reached Iraq. On arrival at his HQ I was amazed to discover that we were to drink English tea and dine on a sumptuous English breakfast whilst a man with a striking white moustache painted the local scene. Maan had created the perfect English club but in the middle of Iraq! He came to visit me from the South of France when I first went into hospital and I am eternally grateful for the support that he has always given me.

There are many others that I would like to thank including all the medical staff at St Mary's and Chelsea and Westminster Hospitals and Farm Lane, as well as my many friends and family across the world. I thank you all for your amazing friendship, generosity and support.

Mahmoud Izadi
London, 2018.

CPSIA information can be obtained
at www.ICGtesting.com
Printed in the USA
LVHW112339140119
603948LV00002B/258/P